The Word of God—
The Word of Peace

The Word of God—
The Word of Peace

Patricia McCarthy, C.N.D.

THE LITURGICAL PRESS
Collegeville, Minnesota

www.litpress.org

Nihil Obstat: Robert C. Harren, *Censor Librorum.*
Imprimatur: ✢ John F. Kinney, Bishop of Saint Cloud, Minnesota, July 21, 2001.

Cover design by Greg Becker. Photo by Cleo Freelance Photography

3   4   5   6   7   8   9

Library of Congress Cataloging-in-Publication Data

McCarthy, Patricia, 1944–
    The word of God—the word of peace / Patricia McCarthy.
    p. cm.
    ISBN 0-8146-2789-7 (alk. paper)
    1. Peace—Biblical teaching. 2. Bible—Criticism, interpretation, etc. I. Title.

BS680.P4 M33 2001
261.8'73—dc21   2001038723

"En estos tiempos son menester amigos fuertes de Dios.
—*Teresa of Avila*

"In these times there is a need for strong friends of God."

To Mackie from Colleen

Contents

Preface

shalom = harmony

This is a book about peace—not the media version of everyone sitting around in designer clothes surrounded by all the desired material possessions. This is a book about peace—the peace of Christ, in Christ, and with Christ. This is a book about peace—peace founded on justice, rooted in freedom, lived in charity, and spoken at the cost of our lives.

The definitive book on peace has already been written through the inspiration of the Holy Spirit. If you are going to read one book on peace, let it be that one book—the Sacred Scriptures. In it God is clear and precise about the message and call of peace. The people of God, on the other hand, aren't so clear and faithful to God's desires for peace. They wheel and deal their way through history, using violence and injustice when it suits them, sometimes even pretending it's God's plan.

The purpose of this book is to encourage, open, and celebrate the word of peace given to us by God in the Scriptures in the time before Christ, and in his own Son after the birth of Christ. As clear as the call to be at peace is, it is not easy to understand or accept. Society and life itself have programmed us to violence, so that we can't even imagine or take seriously the reality that we are called to live in complete peace with all people. The Word of God can penetrate our incredulity, enlighten our vision, and strengthen our resolve to be the people of peace God desires now and has always desired from the beginning of time.

Since peace is lived in the daily circumstances of life, this book highlights the prophets who tried to help the people of their day find peace in the nitty-gritty of life. It is not intended to be a book about the prophets themselves, but rather a book emphasizing the call of prophecy given to each baptized person. "The holy People of God shares also in Christ's prophetic office: it spreads abroad a living witness to him. . . ."[1] Hopefully the commitment to prophetic peace will be highlighted by the teachings of some of the Old and New Testament prophets and, as in all things, illuminated by the life and teachings of our Lord Jesus Christ, the Prince of Peace.

In the first section this book invites us to reflect on God's request. The idea of peace is God's, and God invites others to spread the word. Section Two follows with the response of the peacemaker, the decision to be with God in the work of peace. Section Three brings us to the decisions for peace. When does justice, the foundation of peace, demand that we say yes and when no? The final section deals with the reward of those who are faithful to God's plan. Even the results of peace need scriptural understanding. A life of peace and justice may not match our expectations. Individually and communally we need to immerse ourselves in the desires of God, discern the ways of God for our time and our place, and celebrate with others the cry of God for peace and justice for all people.

Have to disrupt peace to obtain justice

---

[1] Vatican II, Dogmatic Constitution on the Church *(Lumen Gentium),* November 21, 1964, no. 12.

The Request

In the year king Uzziah died, I saw the Lord seated on a high and lofty throne, with the train of his garment filling the temple. Seraphim were stationed above; each of them had six wings: with two they veiled their faces, with two they veiled their feet, and with two they hovered aloft.

"Holy, holy, holy is the LORD of hosts!" they cried one to the other. "All the earth is filled with his glory!" (Isaiah 6:1-3).

Environment matters. The setting of an unusual experience as well as the actual experience is usually remembered. People who survive a natural disaster such as a hurricane or tornado usually recall exactly where they were when it hit. A married couple know when they first met. When the stories are told afterward, the details of the survival or meeting become part of personal legend.

Isaiah is preparing to share his first encounter with God, and he is describing the vision that preceded God's presence. In a way this vision feeds our misconceptions about prophets. We assume that strange physical realities have to occur in order for us to come into the presence of God. The important point of Isaiah's tale is not the fact that unusual phenomena accompany God, but that God is holy and all beings on heaven and earth worship God.

The holiness of God is visible in the seraphim who surround the throne of God. The holiness of God is just as visible in a home or business or airport to those who learn to see. Isaiah's vision was the prelude to an encounter with God, and for that reason a treasure to Isaiah and to God. It was an announcement of the holiness of God, and it was for all the people, not just Isaiah.

As we begin our journey toward peace, Isaiah teaches us three things: God is holy. God reveals this holiness to each of us in a unique way. Our responsibility is to pass on to others the face of God we see.

No one, not even an Isaiah, sees the whole picture. To no human being can the face of God be revealed in its totality. Each of us receives a vision. Through it the Holy touches us and invites us to touch the Holy in each other.

At the sound of that cry, the frame of the door shook and the house was filled with smoke.

Then I said, "Woe is me, I am doomed! For I am a man of unclean lips, living among a people of unclean lips; yet my eyes have seen the King, the LORD of hosts!" Then one of the seraphim flew to me, holding an ember which he had taken with tongs from the altar.

He touched my mouth with it. "See," he said, "now that this has touched your lips, your wickedness is removed, your sin purged."

Then I heard the voice of the Lord saying, "Whom shall I send? Who will go for us?" (Isaiah 6:4-8).

In the Sinai at the time of Moses, Yahweh appeared in the form of fire from the midst of a cloud. Isaiah is experiencing God in a similar way. The smoke of the temple replaces the cloud of Sinai, and the fire of Yahweh is the source of the live coal with which Isaiah is purified.

God is revealing an important reality to Isaiah and to all the people, including us. Our history does not begin with our birth, and our relationship to God does not begin with our first encounter with God. The history of all the people of God is our history and part of our intimate personal relationship with God.

The response of Moses to Yahweh and Yahweh's revelations to Moses are part of Isaiah's call from God. God is letting Isaiah know that the faith of his ancestors is alive in him. The Sinai covenant will continue through Isaiah if he allows God to use him.

There were times in the Exodus when Moses and the chosen people followed God joyfully and in great faith. There were also times when they grumbled and turned away from their God. The people sinned; they were unclean, individually and communally. Isaiah clears the air when he openly admits having the same vacillation of affection toward Yahweh as the desert wanderers did.

God also clears the air, sending his angel to touch Isaiah's tongue with a burning coal, dramatically expressing renewed innocence. God wants Isaiah, and God will brook no resistance, not even the claim of unworthiness. God wants us because God wants us. God loves us because it is the nature of God to love. God will use us because God desires to use us—but only with our free consent.

Freedom is the great sign of God's presence, even more than smoke, fire, and angels. God does not force Isaiah into servitude. God risks vulnerability and makes known to Isaiah the need of God for Isaiah's help. "Whom shall I send? Who will be our messenger?"

The beginning of a relationship with God is the awesome reality that the infinite, all-powerful, almighty God needs us. A vision of seraphim carrying coals is nothing compared to the reality of God desiring us.

Comfort, give comfort to my people,
    says your God.
Speak tenderly to Jerusalem, and proclaim to her
    that her service is at an end,
    her guilt is expiated;
Indeed, she has received from the hand of the LORD
    double for all her sins.

A voice cries out:
In the desert prepare the way of the LORD!
    Make straight in the wasteland a highway for our God!
Every valley shall be filled in,
    every mountain and hill shall be made low;
The rugged land shall be made a plain,
    the rough country, a broad valley . . . .

Go up onto a high mountain,
    Zion, herald of glad tidings;
Cry out at the top of your voice,
    Jerusalem, herald of good news!

> Fear not to cry out
> and say to the cities of Judah:
> Here is your God!
> Here comes with power
> the Lord GOD,
> who rules by his strong arm;
> Here is his reward with him,
> his recompense before him.
> Like a shepherd he feeds his flock;
> in his arms he gathers the lambs,
> Carrying them in his bosom,
> and leading the ewes with care (Isaiah 40:1-4, 9-11).

Even though this Scripture selection is still from the book of Isaiah, its author is not the same person as the one who wrote the earlier chapters. Scripture scholars generally agree that more than one person wrote the book of Isaiah. The first thirty-six chapters are from the prophet Isaiah who was a major religious and political figure of the eighth century before Christ. His disciples seem to have added a few chapters to his original writings. Chapter 40 begins a section that appears to come from the period after the exile of the Jews, which would place it three centuries after the original Isaiah. The style of writing, the teaching content, and the theological development are markedly different from those of Isaiah. So this is not another version of the call to the prophet Isaiah but a unique call to another prophet whose name is not part of Scripture, generally referred to as Second Isaiah.

This is the call to be God's messenger of peace and consolation. The people have suffered terribly. God does not desire suffering. It is never the plan of God but the consequence of sin. The prophet is being asked to go among the sorrowing people and prepare them to receive the good news of God's presence among them.

The absence of fear and the presence of joy mark the proclamation of the kingdom of God. There is no room in God's house for fear and despair. God is a gentle Shepherd who carries the lambs and holds them close to his heart. The messenger of Yahweh must reflect the message itself. If the message is of tenderness and nurturing, then the prophet must be a person of gentleness and compassion, a shepherd to the people.

There is work to be done: the valleys of emptiness need to be filled, the crooked ways of deceit straightened in truth, and the mountains of pride brought low. The call to Second Isaiah is to allow God to work through him. The call to any prophet of God is to allow God to do the converting and the changing of hearts and minds. Planting the seeds, proclaiming the message is the work of the prophet. Fruitfulness and results are the work of God.

> The word of the LORD came to me thus:
> Before I formed you in the womb I knew you,
>> before you were born I dedicated you,
> a prophet to the nations I appointed you (Jeremiah 1:4-5).

God comes to Jeremiah full steam ahead. There is no attempt to control the passion and blessing of Yahweh. Birth is no accident. Each person is part of the design of God; each has a unique story. Jeremiah was chosen by Yahweh even before he came from the womb, before he began to grow within his mother. His existence had been chosen by God from all eternity.

Yahweh knows Jeremiah, not with an intellectual knowledge, but in relationship. The biblical word "know" often means sexual relationship. It is that personal and expansive a word. In this context Yahweh is reaching into the marrow of Jeremiah and claiming him. Jeremiah was chosen before his birth. The choice was to be consecrated, to be a prophet.

Yahweh will allow Jeremiah the opportunity to respond, but the invitation and the first initiative are always Yahweh's. It is God who knows us, chooses us, and stays with us in all things. It is God who desires that we allow ourselves to be "appointed as prophets to the nations."

By our baptism each of us is called to be prophet, priest, and king. So many Christians today think that holiness is about being good more times than being bad, and hoping God is a merciful accountant. Religion is about love, and the start of religion is God's love for each person. God's expectations and dreams for each of us far exceed the wildest imaginings of the most doting parent.

God sends each of us to be a spokesperson of the word of God for all the nations. No president, ambassador, statesperson, bishop, or international figure has a greater responsibility than one called to be God's representative on earth. God is choosing us from all eternity, consecrating us from the first moment of our existence, to proclaim the word of God to all nations.

Fidelity to God's ways and perseverance in a life committed to justice and lived in peace begin with the knowledge of God's love. In the deepest part of our being there must be the certitude that God loves us and trusts us so much that we are necessary for the work of God to continue in our day.

Then the LORD extended his hand and touched my mouth, saying,
See, I place my words in your mouth!
This day I set you
over nations and over kingdoms,
To root up and to tear down,
to destroy and to demolish,
to build and to plant (Jeremiah 1:9-10).

God reaches out to touch Jeremiah. It is incredible, improbable, unimaginable that the hand of God would touch a human person in this way. God, who needs nothing or no one, is allowing Jeremiah to be needed by God.

A more impersonal God, a less affectionate God, perhaps would command or dictate divine plans and desires. But Jeremiah's God, the God of the Hebrew people and our God, goes for hands-on contact. No intermediary here! And the touch is on the mouth. Intimacy is revealed in these words. In Western culture strangers can touch hands. It is a way of acknowledging meeting someone or closing a deal. But only an intimate friend can touch the mouth of another. It is God's words that are placed in the mouth of Jeremiah and in the mouth of every person who accepts the same challenge as Jeremiah did—the challenge to be touched by God for God's purposes.

Jeremiah was going to be used in ways he never would have chosen himself. A gentle man, he was sent to disturb his people's mediocrity, which was leading to their own destruction. Jeremiah had a tough message to preach, but it was the message God asked him to preach. Prophets in every age are called to proclaim God's message, which is not the one society wants to hear. It may be the salvation message, but due to human weakness and reluctance to change, few want to hear it if it means disturbing their current pattern of living.

God knew that it would be necessary for Jeremiah to remember the touch of God's hands in the dark hours when everyone seemed to turn against him and the message of God he was trying to proclaim. The personal touch of his mouth by Yahweh precedes Jeremiah's proclamation of the word of God. This intimate moment will sustain him when the rejection by his own people would make the word of God feel like dust in his mouth.

You duped me, O LORD, and I let myself be duped;
  you were too strong for me, and you triumphed.
All the day I am an object of laughter;
  everyone mocks me (Jeremiah 20:7).

There are two key elements to this cry from Jeremiah: the seduction by God and the acquiescence of Jeremiah. For now let us reflect on God's part—the seduction of a prophet. This is a powerful statement from Jeremiah. It comes after he has begun living his role as prophet. In fact, it comes immediately after he has been arrested and tortured for proclaiming the word of God (Jeremiah 20:1, 2).

Therefore, this is no early romantic version of Jeremiah's relationship with Yahweh. Jeremiah has experienced the consequences of fidelity in the face of political and social corruption. He has been tried and tested in the jail of suffering. And he comes out crying that God has seduced him. Jeremiah has experienced God's love to such a degree that he cannot refuse it. He doesn't say that God commanded him or God threatened him. Jeremiah expresses no fear; rather he admits freely that God has swept him off his feet with passion, and Jeremiah is unable and unwilling to resist.

Hollywood films constantly try to portray this kind of love. Their attempts are futile. God is love and God is the greatest lover of all time. Only God can produce and direct such a love scene. Jeremiah knows this. In spite of the dire consequences of this love, that is, jail and torture, Jeremiah rejoices in it. The passion of God is so great that it overwhelms resistance. In the face of the reality that has happened because of his proclaiming Yahweh's words, Jeremiah proclaims his own word of love and passion.

Crises sift out weak motivations and superficial emotional support. If love persists, it must be total surrender. The call of the prophet, the call of the one chosen to proclaim the peace of God to all people is the call to complete abandonment in love to the God of love. Jeremiah grasped God's love for him to the point where Jeremiah could not do anything but accept being taken. His example reveals that getting involved with God goes beyond the rational, deliberate choice. It gets into life-surging passion from which there is no turning back.

Hear this word, O men of Israel, that the LORD pronounces over you, over the whole family that I brought up from the land of Egypt:
>   You alone have I favored,
>   more than all the families of the earth (Amos 3:1, 2).

The shepherd Amos was called from his flock to speak God's word to a wealthy nation whose inhabitants were living a corrupt, materialistic, selfish lifestyle. In his direct approach and simple language, Amos makes it perfectly clear that he is preaching God's word, not his own. Paying little attention to his own spiritual history, Amos emphasizes the call of Yahweh to the whole nation of Israel.

Yahweh approaches Israel as a whole with the same intimate cry for union with which he seduces individuals. It is always the same: the individual and the communal call intricately, eternally bound together. "You alone of all the families of earth, have I acknowledged." Biblical knowledge of someone means love and choice. God has chosen Israel to be special, to be treasured, to be loved.

Amos helps us to see the community aspect of a personal call from God. It is impossible to hear the word of God just for ourselves or to hear it and not share it with others. Relationship is the nature of God. Since the birth of Christ we know that our God is a God of relationship: Father, Son, and Spirit. But even at the time of Amos, centuries before the Incarnation, Yahweh is preparing the people.

Christ will tell us that as he and the Father are one, so are we one with them and with one another (John 17:11). Through Amos, Yahweh reveals that he acknowledges Israel. He loves Israel. He chooses Israel. Yahweh's people are bound to one another by their relationship with God.

The implications are astounding. To be chosen as a people surely determines the quality of interpersonal relations. In more simple language, how could someone chosen by God kill, injure, ignore, or mistreat any other person also chosen by God? Living in peace with others is not merely the effect of being a generous, loving person. Living in peace is the only way consistent with the call of God. God has called us as a people. To try to separate out some persons is a denial of the design of God and a refusal to accept the call of God to ourselves and to others.

Son of man, stand up! I wish to speak with you. As he spoke to me, spirit entered into me and set me on my feet, and I heard the one who was speaking say to me: Son of man, I am sending you to the Israelites, rebels who have rebelled against me; they and their fathers have revolted against me to this very day. Hard of face and obstinate of heart are they to whom I am sending you. But you shall say to them: Thus says the Lord GOD! And whether they heed or resist—for they are a rebellious house—they shall know that a prophet has been among them. But as for you, son of man, fear neither them nor their words when they contradict you and reject you, and when you sit on scorpions. Neither fear their words nor be dismayed at their looks, for they are a rebellious house. [But speak my words to them, whether they heed or resist, for they are rebellious.] As for you, son of man, obey me when I speak to you: be not rebellious like this house of rebellion, but open your mouth and eat what I shall give you.

It was then I saw a hand stretched out to me, in which was a written scroll which he unrolled before me. It was covered with writing front and back, and written on it was: Lamentation and wailing and woe!

He said to me: Son of man, eat what is before you; eat this scroll, then go, speak to the house of Israel. So I opened my mouth and he gave me the scroll to eat (Ezekiel 2:1-10; 3:1-2).

What an awesome vision introduces Ezekiel to God's plan for him. Yahweh clarifies who is God and who is not. "Son of man" is the address God uses to Ezekiel. The words convey the infinite distance between God and humans. This is the first time this expression appears in Scripture. In the future Jesus will assume this title for himself, laying claim to be the Messiah. Jesus crossed that unbreachable gap between Creator and creature and brought us along with him.

But that is for the future. For now Ezekiel is being made aware of how impossible it is for a mortal to approach God. God commands Ezekiel to "stand up!" How wonderful that he is called to stand in the presence of God! This is the essence of the call: to stand before God and to be sent out to proclaim the word of God.

Yahweh's solemn proclamation states emphatically that the message is to be preached whether people listen or not. Success is never the measure of the prophet, only fidelity to the word. Society never accepts the one who speaks for God and of God. No matter, the message must be preached.

The call to Ezekiel is clear. The word of God is to be his nourishment and proclaiming it his mission. Yahweh gives Ezekiel the word to eat. "Eat what is given to you." Inherent in the call is the promise that God is sufficient for life itself. Later on we hear Christ telling us, "Take and eat." As the body needs to eat to live, so does our spirit need to eat the word of God to live. The mission of every Christian begins with deep acceptance of the reality that God is sufficient for us. We don't need anything else.

In the third year of the reign of Jehoiakim, king of Judah, King Nebuchadnezzar of Babylon came and laid siege to Jerusalem. . . .

The king told Ashpenaz, his chief chamberlain, to bring in some of the Israelites of royal blood and of the nobility, young men without any defect, handsome, intelligent and wise, quick to learn, and prudent in judgment, such as could take their place in the king's palace; they were to be taught the language and literature of the Chaldeans . . . . Among these were men of Judah: Daniel, Hananiah, Mishael, and Azariah. The chief chamberlain changed their names: Daniel to Belteshazzar, Hananiah to Shadrach, Mishael to Meshach, and Azariah to Abednego.

But Daniel was resolved not to defile himself with the king's food or wine; so he begged the chief chamberlain to spare him this defilement. Though God had given Daniel the favor and sympathy of the chief chamberlain, he nevertheless said to Daniel, "I am afraid of my lord the king; it is he who allotted your food and drink. If he sees that you look wretched by comparison with the other young men of your age, you will endanger my life with the king." Then Daniel said to the steward whom the chief chamberlain had put in charge of Daniel, Hananiah, Mishael, and Azariah, "Please test your servants for ten days. Give us vegetables to eat and water to drink. Then see how we look in comparison with the other young men who eat from the royal table, and treat your servants according to what you see."

He acceded to this request, and tested them for ten days; after ten days they looked healthier and better fed than any of the young men who ate from the royal table. So the steward continued to take away the food and wine they were to receive, and gave them vegetables.

To these four young men God gave knowledge and proficiency in all literature and science, and to Daniel the understanding of all visions and dreams (Daniel 1:1, 3-4, 6-17).

Daniel's call from God is hidden within the daily circumstances of Daniel's life. The conquering king is looking for smart, good-looking young men to work in his service. So Daniel and his friends become forced laborers at an enemy's bidding. And in the midst of the catastrophe, God raises up a prophet.

Yahweh, who never abandons his people, reaches into the lap of the enemy and rescues Daniel without removing him. God is revealing the inability of anyone to foil the divine designs. God wants to use Daniel and will do so, regardless of obstacles. What is expected of Daniel is faith.

This story of the hidden call of Daniel resembles the call so many receive: to find God even when life seems to have blocked God from our sight. We don't have the words of God calling Daniel, nor, at this early point in his life, do we have the visions of Daniel. They will come later. For now we have what Daniel has—a heritage of faith in Yahweh.

The call to Daniel comes through his heritage. Daniel hears it in his attempt to be faithful to the dietary laws of his people. Of course, for the Israelites at that time, the dietary laws were a sign of their worship of God. To abandon the laws was to abandon God. Daniel's fidelity to the law was a sign of his recognition of Yahweh as the one true God.

A king's orders could not be obeyed at the expense of disobeying God's. Scripture begins the story of Daniel without any sense of uniqueness to his call. Daniel is being asked to be faithful in the same way that every other Israelite is asked: to observe the laws of their faith. In Daniel's case, he risks his life by disobeying the king's orders. Daniel trusts God, and this act inaugurates the extraordinary love story between God and Daniel.

> Therefore you shall have night, not vision,
>   darkness, not divination;
> The sun shall go down upon the prophets,
>   and the day shall be dark for them.
> Then shall the seers be put to shame,
>   and the diviners confounded;
> They shall cover their lips, all of them,
>   because there is no answer from God.
> But as for me, I am filled with power,
>   with the spirit of the LORD,
>   with authority and with might;
> To declare to Jacob his crimes
>   and to Israel his sins (Micah 3:6-8).

The Sacred Scriptures give nothing specific of Micah's life and call, but they do reveal his strong sense of having been chosen by God. The fervor of his words conveys the conviction of his heart. Micah possesses that inner certitude common to the friends of God. Jesus has it when he confronts Pilate (John 19:9-11), and Paul when he lays claim to his role as apostle of Christ (1 Corinthians 9:1).

Anyone can be deceived; anyone can be blinded to the truth. It is possible for well-intentioned people to follow the wrong path. Micah accepts this reality in life and acknowledges the presence of false prophets who lead others astray. How is one to know the false from the true? There is the obvious answer to this: by their fruit you know them.[1] Joy, peace, kindness, perseverance, etc.—all are signs of the presence of God. Fear, revenge, self-righteousness, violence, greed, etc.—all are signs of the absence of God.

Beyond and before these external witnesses to truth, the friend of God just knows the call to be true. Micah rails against the false prophet and with the boldness of God proclaims, "Not so with me." He is convinced beyond doubt, beyond fear, that he is chosen by God and sent by God. The certitude comes from his relationship with God. Micah knows God and God knows Micah. God is with Micah. "I am filled with power, with the spirit of the LORD."

Yahweh alone is Micah's strength, and the Spirit of the Lord fills Micah's own spirit as completely as each breath he draws fills his body. Breath is the vital life source. "The LORD God formed man out of the clay of the ground and blew into his nostrils the breath of life, and so man became a living being" (Genesis 2:7). When Christ came, he revealed the fullness of our union with God in Christ. Micah is expressing that union in as complete a way as a human being can. If our breath is God's breath, if God lives in us, then we live only in God and for God. Faith understood in this way is neither a set of rules nor tenets of belief. Faith is awareness of the abiding, indwelling, sustaining presence of God.

Micah proclaims his call and celebrates his all-consuming union with Yahweh, the prerequisite to being the spokesperson of God.

---

[1] See Matthew 12:33; Galatians 5:22-23; Luke 7:43-45.

In the beginning of the LORD's speaking to Hosea, the LORD said to Hosea:
> Go, take a harlot wife and harlot's children,
>   for the land gives itself to harlotry,
>   turning away from the LORD.

So he went and took Gomer, the daughter of Diblaim; and she conceived and bore him a son. Then the LORD said to him:
> Give him the name Jezreel,
>   for in a little while
> I will punish the house of Jehu
>   for the bloodshed at Jezreel
> And bring to an end the kingdom
>   of the house of Israel;
> On that day I will break the bow of Israel
>   in the valley of Jezreel.

When she conceived again and bore a daughter, the LORD said to him:
> Give her the name Lo-ruhama;
> I no longer feel pity for the house of Israel:
>   rather, I abhor them utterly.
> Yet for the house of Judah I feel pity;
>   I will save them by the LORD, their God;
> But I will not save them by war,
>   by sword or bow, by horses or horsemen.

After she weaned Lo-ruhama, she conceived and bore a son. Then the LORD said:
> Give him the name Lo-ammi,
>   for you are not my people,
>   and I will not be your God (Hosea 1:2-9).

Unfortunately the word of Yahweh did not come to Hosea in a vision or in symbolism. It came through the heartbreaking personal experience of an unfaithful wife. Yahweh goes into the woundedness of Hosea, whose wife has borne him three children but cannot give him her own fidelity. This shattered relationship is the ground into which God will sow hope and promise for Hosea and through him for all of Israel.

Yahweh doesn't have to wait for perfect people in perfect situations to reveal the almighty plan of God. Hosea takes daily life, so cruel and disturbing in his case, and allows God room to heal and console and eventually to conquer. Hosea could, by law, have put away his wife or had her stoned. He could have wallowed in the hopelessness of his pathetic marriage. His pain could have consumed all his psyche, energy, and hope. Instead Hosea keeps his broken heart open to God and to his wife. When Yahweh first spoke to Hosea, life was bleak. In Jesus' time he would say that he came for the sinner and the lost sheep of Israel. What sounds so consoling in Jesus' mouth is a harsh reality. God's word called Hosea to forgive his wife as Yahweh would forgive the unfaithful Israelites.

For a man in Hosea's culture and time, as is still the case, a faithless wife was a great insult to his manhood. The standard for sexual purity for women was higher than it was for men. For this biased reason, Hosea's story is all the more shocking for his culture. The man was not expected to overlook the infidelity of his wife; he was meant to banish her and denounce her publicly.

In the midst of this mess, the word of God finds Hosea ready and willing to speak beyond his pain for the sake of his God. For those who protest that the Hebrew Scriptures allow for violence, the story of Hosea's call is a clear rebuttal to that claim. God will use this forgiving love of Hosea to reveal the forgiving love of Yahweh for his unfaithful Israel. Through the agony of a shattered marital relationship, Yahweh uses the sacred, intimate love of marriage as a symbol of his own love for the chosen ones.

I will espouse you to me forever:
    I will espouse you in right and in justice,
      in love and in mercy;
    I will espouse you in fidelity,
    and you shall know the LORD (Hosea 2:21-22).

Usually we think of the call of the prophet in terms of those righteous men and women of God who were listening to, and open to at least hear, the voice of God. This passage from Hosea is the call to the unfaithful, to the sinner. This is an important aspect of the Gospel message, namely, that all people are called—the saint and the sinner. And all are called in love.

Yahweh promises to "espouse you to me forever." Yahweh is speaking to the unfaithful bride, Israel. Like the father of the prodigal son story will do later, there is no remonstrance. Only the declaration of intimate love accompanies the call to return.

Yet the words speak of contractual commitment. Betrothal, faithfulness, tenderness, integrity, justice—all these words imply a sense of mutuality. The forgiveness of God is unconditional and the fidelity of God is everlasting, but the individual or the people involved in this love affair with God must freely surrender. Their fidelity and integrity are a necessary part of the union.

Even redemption and forgiveness of sin are not forced on anyone. There is always the request to listen, to accept, to obey, to give God primacy in all things and among all people. The call is not denied to those who appear to be at high risk of turning away; the unfaithful wife is sought in the desert. She is cajoled and courted, showered with promises of love. This is all part of the call. In the final analysis, the call comes from the covenantal relationship of God with the chosen people, yet far surpasses it.

When the Israelites failed to live up to their part of the bargain with God, God still loved and pursued them. He continued to invite them to know the Lord, just as Hosea continued to invite his unfaithful wife to be loved intimately. God's call reaches into the most abandoned dregs of humanity, relentlessly searching for love. No one is ever worthy of the call of God, and no one is deemed unworthy by God.

In the days of Herod, King of Judea, there was a priest named Zechariah of the priestly division of Abijah; his wife was from the daughters of Aaron, and her name was Elizabeth. Both were righteous in the eyes of God, observing all the commandments and ordinances of the Lord blamelessly. But they had no child, because Elizabeth was barren and both were advanced in years. Once when he was serving as priest in his division's turn before God, according to the practice of the priestly service, he was chosen by lot to enter the sanctuary of the Lord to burn incense. Then, when the whole assembly of the people was praying outside at the hour of the incense offering, the angel of the Lord appeared to him, standing at the right of the altar of incense. Zechariah was troubled by what he saw, and fear came upon him. But the angel said to him, "Do not be afraid, Zechariah, because your prayer has been heard. Your wife Elizabeth will bear you a son, and you shall name him John. And you will have joy and gladness, and many will rejoice at his birth, for he will be great in the sight of [the] Lord. He will drink neither wine nor strong drink. He will be filled with the holy Spirit even from his mother's womb, and he will turn many of the children of Israel to the Lord their God. He will go before him in the spirit and power of Elijah to turn the hearts of fathers toward children and the disobedient to the understanding of the righteous, to prepare a people fit for the Lord" (Luke 1:5-17).

The birth announcement of John the Baptist is intertwined with the continuing call to Zechariah. Long before this incident Zechariah had heard God's call, so much so that he was a member of the priestly group. He was performing the duties of his office when the angel of the Lord interrupted him with the news flash about his future son. Zechariah was praying to God and offering incense, but he never expected God to call in the way he did.

Most of us are like Zechariah. God surprises us often, and we seem to be always looking in the opposite direction from where God comes. There is one initial call from God, but there are many other calls within the call as life progresses. Zechariah experienced one with the appearance of the angel bearing God's plans for him and Elizabeth.

The promise of a son carries with it God's plans for the son. John the Baptist's vocational call is proclaimed before his conception. He will be "great in the sight of the Lord," "filled with the holy Spirit," and will bring people back to their God.

Unique as each call is, there is always the consistent theme of choice and favor for the sake of the kingdom. Jesus himself said of John: ". . . among those born of women there has been none greater" (Matthew 11:11), and the credit is clearly given to the Holy Spirit. What makes a prophet the voice of God is the presence of the Spirit of God. John was great because he allowed God to use him freely.

Scripture explicitly acknowledges the choice of John from his conception. The events of John's conception itself are unusual, but the reality of being called from the first moment of existence isn't. Each of us is called as early and as completely as John was called. Most of our parents knew of our expected birth from a doctor rather than an angel, but that does not preclude our being chosen by God from all eternity. And the joy and celebration that accompanied John's announcement are a sign of the rejoicing that God celebrates in each new life.

> In the sixth month, the angel Gabriel was sent from God to a town of Galilee called Nazareth, to a virgin betrothed to a man named Joseph, of the house of David, and the virgin's name was Mary. And coming to her, he said, "Hail, favored one! The Lord is with you." But she was greatly troubled at what was said and pondered what sort of greeting this might be. Then the angel said to her, "Do not be afraid, Mary, for you have found favor with God. Behold, you will conceive in your womb and bear a son, and you shall name him Jesus. He will be great and will be called Son of the Most High, and the Lord God will give him the throne of David his father, and he will rule over the house of Jacob forever, and of his kingdom there will be no end." But Mary said to the angel, "How can this be, since I have no relations with a man?" And the angel said to her in reply, "The holy Spirit will come upon you, and the power of the Most High will overshadow you. Therefore the child to be born will be called holy, the Son of God. And behold, Elizabeth, your relative, has also conceived a son in her old age, and this is the sixth month for her who was called barren; for nothing will be impossible for God" (Luke 1:26-37).

"Annunciation" is the word used to describe Mary's call from God. What a request! Imagine God, knowing from all eternity that redemption would be accomplished, asking the cooperation of a human being to bring it about! Almighty God is asking a teenage girl from the Jordan area if she will bear the Son of God. An angel is sent down, a messenger. He greets Mary, "The Lord is with you." A simple statement holding the promise of the ages. Mary is one of a whole people blessed by God, a people who know that all that is necessary is that God be present. All other things are passing and trivial. The presence of God is the pearl of great price Jesus would talk about years after this moment of conception. In every prophetic call is the assurance of the abiding presence of God. It may not always be stated, but it is integral to the call.

The Holy Spirit will do the impossible if the young girl will agree. What kind of a God have we who lets divine plans be dependent upon human involvement? This magnificent story of God's intervention and request is exactly the same story as experienced by every baptized person. Each is asked to bear the Christ, the Son of the living God. The details of time and space vary, but the essence of humanity bearing divinity endures.

History knows the answer, but the moment before the answer, the moment when the question of eternity hung in time—this is the prophetic moment. Mary was asked by God to enter into the unknown, relying solely on God. In every person's call from God, the same situation exists. Circumstances are different, but the players and rules are always the same. God asks individuals for total surrender and complete abandonment for the sake of the work of God on this earth. The request can seem disturbing at first, but trust in God can replace fear. It usually seems improbable, but "nothing will be impossible for God."

In those days a decree went out from Caesar Augustus that the whole world should be enrolled. This was the first enrollment, when Quirinius was governor of Syria. So all went to be enrolled, each to his own town. And Joseph too went up from Galilee from the town of Nazareth to Judea, to the city of David that is called Bethlehem, because he was of the house and family of David, to be enrolled with Mary, his betrothed, who was with child. While they were there, the time came for her to have her child, and she gave birth to her firstborn son. She wrapped him in swaddling

clothes and laid him in a manger, because there was no room for
them in the inn (Luke 2:1-7).

Angels visited both Mary and Joseph to announce the conception of Christ. The birth narrative is structured so that it is clear
that this Christ is the Messiah and Lord. The city of Bethlehem,
the manger, the shepherds are all part of the story, so that Jesus is
seen as the promised one, the continuation and fulfillment of the
covenant. Bethlehem is the city of David when he was a young
shepherd. It was his city when he was powerless and young. Jerusalem was his city when he was rich and powerful. Bethlehem, the
small, forgotten city, was foretold by Micah to be the birthplace of
the Messiah (see Micah 5:1). The manger image is from Isaiah
(Isaiah 1:3), a sign of the recognition of the Messiah by the people.

As an adult, Jesus will clarify in both word and deed how he
is the Messiah. He will lay claim to his oneness with the Father,
and he will proclaim that his only desire is to do the will of the
Father. We will see in Jesus the perfection of the call we all receive: to be united with God and to bring others to the same
union.

The birth story holds this in embryo. The poverty and humility of the life chosen for the Son of God and the rejection he
was to encounter are all in the Bethlehem scene. It was written
from the perspective of Calvary, connecting the Hebrew law and
prophets to the Gospel. From a birth in a remote city a child is
born who is the fulfillment of all the promises of Yahweh. The
birth is announced to shepherds and magi (Luke 2:8-20;
Matthew 2:1-12). Angels sing of peace and praise.

Every prophet, that is, every baptized Christian, needs to
find his or her own call in the birth of Jesus. The call will be total,
to be revealed over a lifetime, as Jesus' call was revealed over his
lifetime. The sign is, first, recognition of this child as Savior and,
then, willingness to announce his life and message to others.

Now there were shepherds in that region living in the fields and
keeping the night watch over their flock. The angel of the Lord appeared to them and the glory of the Lord shone around them, and

they were struck with great fear. The angel said to them, "Do not be afraid; for behold, I proclaim to you good news of great joy that will be for all the people. For today in the city of David a savior has been born for you who is Messiah and Lord. And this will be a sign for you: you will find an infant wrapped in swaddling clothes and lying in a manger." And suddenly there was a multitude of the heavenly host with the angel, praising God and saying:
"Glory to God in the highest
and on earth peace to those on whom his favor rests" (Luke 2:8-14).

Terror often accompanies the divine intervention of God. Strange, isn't it? Psychologists observe that most people stay in unproductive and unhealthy situations rather than dare to change. It takes courage to change, because there is always the risk of the unknown. God desires our conversion for our sake as well as for the kingdom's sake. God wants us to change to free us from the darkness.

The angels announce to the shepherds the kingdom message: the Christ is born; great joy is here for all the people. Praise to God and peace among us. From these first Gospel verses the essence of peace is clear. It is not merely a by-product of the presence of Christ. It is the person of Christ himself. Peace, love, joy, praise are who Christ is. It is the Savior's reality, never to be separated from him. We cannot associate our Lord with violence, hatred, despair, or idolatry.

Who among us has not suffered from these evils? The shepherds in Luke's Gospel had known pain from all the same social sins. In a flash of angelic song, they hear another voice, the one of peace, love, joy, and praise. Like us, they were frightened at the promise of redemption, so used to violence that any other way is too great a stretch of the imagination. More than a creative imagination is at stake here—it is the raw call of faith to believe in Christ as Savior. A baby in swaddling clothes doesn't look much like a redeemer. The way of peace doesn't look viable in the face of evil. And yet it is the announcement of the angels, the announcement of the Savior. Now it is up to the shepherds to choose to hear the message and believe or to keep on with business as usual.

The first step into peace is to hear the announcement of the Prince of Peace, Jesus Christ. Faith alone hears the call to enter into the new way of living, the way transformed by the incarnation of Jesus Christ.

As he was walking by the Sea of Galilee, he saw two brothers, Simon who is called Peter, and his brother Andrew, casting a net into the sea; they were fishermen. He said to them, "Come after me, and I will make you fishers of men. . . ." He walked along from there and saw two other brothers, James, the son of Zebedee, and his brother John. They were in a boat, with their father Zebedee, mending their nets. He called them . . . (Matthew 4:18, 19, 21).

As Jesus passed on from there, he saw a man named Matthew sitting at the customs post. He said to him, "Follow me" (Matthew 9:9).

Simon and Andrew were fishing, casting out their nets when Jesus walked up to them. He was direct: "Come after me, and I will make you fishers of men." James and John were mending their nets with their father. Jesus called them too. Matthew was a tax collector, working his booth on the public road. He heard the same call: "Follow me." No extraordinary phenomenon, no visible miracles, no angelic song or lights in the sky.

Jesus chose these men, two sets of brothers and a tax collector. Something in them attracted Jesus, and something in Jesus attracted Simon, Andrew, James, John, and Matthew. We know it was the Holy Spirit but they didn't. They saw only Jesus. Something in him was irresistible, exciting. They wanted to be with him. Long before theology and church practices, there was Jesus. None of us is called to an institution, even to a creed. Like these first apostles, we are called to Jesus. We are called to surrender to the mutual attraction, to go with the pull of Jesus.

Jesus will find us in the everyday reality of our work and home. He will search for us while we go about the ordinary, mundane things that fill our days. He will come as he did to the apostles—personally and simply. He will ask us to believe he is worth following, to leave the things that consume our energy, even the things that seem to be essential. Jesus asks us to focus on him and to dare to take our eyes off our precious possessions. If we look, we may discover what the apostles discovered. The face of Christ dwarfs all other things. The call to follow him comes as the greatest gift ever offered. Simon and Andrew, James and John, and Matthew recognized the pearl of great price in the young Arab man calling them. They dared to risk everything for it.

Now someone approached him and said, "Teacher, what good must I do to gain eternal life?" He answered him, "Why do you ask me about the good? There is only One who is good. If you wish to enter into life, keep the commandments." He asked him, "Which ones?" And Jesus replied, "'You shall not kill; you shall not commit adultery; you shall not steal; you shall not bear false witness; honor your father and your mother'; and 'you shall love your neighbor as yourself.'" The young man said to him, "All of these I have observed. What do I still lack?" Jesus said to him, "If you wish to be perfect, go, sell what you have and give to [the] poor, and you will have treasure in heaven. Then come, follow me" (Matthew 19:16-21).

A discussion of faith is far from a commitment of faith. The rich young man enters into discussion with Jesus about faith. He asks what to do to guarantee life with God for all eternity. Jesus repeats the basic principles of the Hebrew faith: the commandments. The young man knows there is more to life than the Decalogue. He has kept these commandments from his youth. What else is there? Then Jesus looks on him with love and asks him to leave everything and follow him.

All through the Hebrew Scriptures the story is the same. From the time of Abraham the call is to love God totally. "Go forth from the land of your kinsfolk and from your father's house to a land I will show you" (Genesis 12:1). Our God is a demanding God, asking everything from those chosen. The rich young man was on the brink of realizing that religion isn't a cloak to be put on or off at will but a complete embrace of a God who first embraced him. He was at the crucial crossroads of moving from a child's faith based on rules to an adult's faith of relationship.

Jesus stood with him and would have stayed with him forever, but the young man had to accept Jesus. In this scene Jesus calls and waits. He loves the young man, desires him, and asks him to love back. What began as discussion continues as intimate exchange. Now the young man is faced with a choice: to stay in mediocrity or to embrace the fullness of life. It is a difficult choice if the focus is on the apparent cost, the leaving of material possessions; it is a leap of joy if the focus is on Jesus.

Every adult Christian must make the decision the young man faced. It is possible to cruise through one's faith. It is the superficial way of keeping religious customs and rules. Then the day comes when Christ stands in front of us in such a way that we see there is an opportunity for more. Something in us soars at the sight of Jesus. At the same time we recognize that something must be left behind to delve into a deeper relationship. The call is to trust Jesus totally and to love him as he loves. Jesus offers love and then waits—for the rich young man and for us.

Now Saul, still breathing murderous threats against the disciples of the Lord, went to the high priest and asked him for letters to the synagogues in Damascus, that, if he should find any men or women who belonged to the Way, he might bring them back to Jerusalem in chains. On his journey, as he was nearing Damascus, a light from the sky suddenly flashed around him. He fell to the ground and heard a voice saying to him, "Saul, Saul, why are you persecuting me?" He said, "Who are you, sir?" The reply came, "I am Jesus, whom you are persecuting. Now get up and go into the city and you will be told what you must do." The men who were traveling with him stood speechless, for they heard the voice but could see no one. Saul got up from the ground, but when he opened his eyes he could see nothing; so they led him by the hand and brought him to Damascus. For three days he was unable to see, and he neither ate nor drank (Acts 9:1-9).

Saul was knocked to the ground by the call from Christ. Sometimes it happens like that. A crisis precipitates faith. Jesus came to Paul in the disguise of the Christians he was persecuting.

Paul was a temple-going Jew, a Pharisee by training. He was so zealous that he was intent on persecuting any of those who were in that new sect of Jesus' followers. He saw those who were different as a threat.

Paul had his handle on God, and he was violent in protecting that control. Jesus loved Paul, even while Paul was a long way off. Jesus shattered Paul's reality and comfort. Jesus took on the face of those who suffer; he told Paul he was one with them and they with him.

Now Paul is indeed blind. Actually he has not seen for a long time. He must choose to see in the darkness. He must choose to believe in the light when it is covered. How many of us suffer the blindness of Paul! We look for God in our shrines and false images; we try to limit God to our religious acts and words. Yet Christ escapes from the narrow cell we build for him. Jesus comes in the disturbing presence of the oppressed and abused of every time and place. His presence overwhelms our resistance and breaks through our reserve. Like Paul, we find ourselves face to face with an unknown God.

The moment of call can also be the moment of awareness of sin. The light of Christ penetrates the darkness and reveals the hidden evil. Christ is love, so his presence cannot abide the presence of evil. Paul was shocked to hear that he was persecuting Christ. Now Paul must be led by another and wait until he knows how to respond. The first part of a journey from evil to good, from darkness to light, is to admit the sin. Paul is at that part of his journey. He fasts and surely prays until he can move from hatred to love, until he can see with the eyes of Christ, until the scales of his own self-righteousness can fall off.

SECTION TWO

The Response

Then I heard the voice of the Lord saying, "Whom shall I send?
Who will go for us?" "Here I am," I said; "send me!" And he
replied: Go and say to this people:
   Listen carefully, but you shall not understand!
   Look intently, but you shall know nothing! (Isaiah 6:8-9).

Readiness, availability, and vulnerability characterize the direct, confident response of Isaiah to his God's need for a messenger. Isaiah is not the first in Scripture to so easily and completely
abandon himself. Abraham was also generous and faith-filled
(Genesis 12:1-4). David, despite all his misguided ambitions for
power and his propensity to lust, wrote psalm after psalm of surrender to a loving God. Tobias and Sarah from different places si-
multaneously placed themselves in God's hands; and an angel of
God brought them together to share and celebrate that trust
through human love (Book of Tobit). Throughout history people
of faith fall in love with God, hear the call, and answer in faith and
joy. Francis of Assisi threw away his material possessions to rebuild
the house of God. Ignatius of Loyola surrendered his weapons in a
greater surrender of heart to lead people not in battle but in faith.
Mother Teresa said her yes by picking up the dying in the streets.
Dorothy Day did the same thing in New York. Mohandas Gandhi
wanted his whole life to be a cry for God's truth. He died with the
name of God on his lips.

Though many have done it, surrender to God still is an
awesome experience to contemplate, let alone to embrace. Isaiah
takes the plunge. He exercises the greatest attribute of humanity—

free choice. Enthusiastically Isaiah responds. And within the simplicity of the response, the person of Isaiah is revealed.

Isaiah is at home in his own skin; he knows who he is. He can stand in his own truth and proclaim to God: "Here I am." Isaiah understands that God delights in our being and desires that we confidently proclaim our very existence. Before we can give ourselves to God or to any other person, we must possess ourselves. God's gift of creation of each of us is a treasure to receive, acknowledge, and discover.

Isaiah exists in time and place, and he knows that. He is not being swept along in life without a sense of identity or purpose. He first announces that he is present to himself and then to his God. "Send me." Amazing courage in this answer to Yahweh's plea! Isaiah enters fully into God's employ. Whatever God asks, Isaiah will embrace. Wherever God sends him, Isaiah will go. However long the journey, Isaiah will persevere.

> A voice says, "Cry out!"
> I answer, "What shall I cry out?" (Isaiah 40:6).

The response of the prophet called Second Isaiah, because he came centuries after Isaiah, is simple and direct. He asks a question of clarification, not of resistance. Second Isaiah doesn't seem to hesitate to acquiesce to God's desire, but he just isn't sure what God wants him to do or say.

God often begins working in a soul without apparent clarity. God is clear but the person doesn't comprehend the message totally. God desires and calls the person to assist in the work of salvation, to bring the Good News to all people. Something stirs in the person, a sense of freedom and joy mixed with insecurity and confusion. Eagerly a positive response is made in the heart while a question blurts from the mouth.

Second Isaiah is not hesitating to follow God's call, "Cry!" He responds: "What shall I cry?" Here is an ordinary man being asked to console the people of God, to prepare for the coming of God, to fill the valleys and straighten the paths, to proclaim the

message to all Jerusalem. It takes extraordinary courage to accept
that challenge. Not many would feel capable of applying for the
job of joyful messenger of the Lord.

Second Isaiah takes a necessary step along the road of
preaching peace. He accepts the call from God and responds
without being held back by personal inadequacies. If any of us
hear God calling us to be proclaimers of the kingdom of God, the
kingdom of presence and peace, and stop to check out our worthiness, we will never move further. Worthiness is not a part of
our response to God. None of us is worthy, none able, none capable of being a spokesperson for God. God alone is holy; God's
message alone is true. And God trusts us with this message. All
we have to do is to be willing to let God use us, vulnerable to be
filled with the goodness of God.

If we look at the message of peace and say, "It is impossible
and I cannot proclaim it," then we are stopping at human limitations. We are letting life as we know it be our standard rather
than life as God intends us to experience it. A step toward crying
God's message of peace is to come before God and ask, "What
shall I say?" Then just wait and listen.

This is the word of the LORD that came to Jonah, son of Amittai:
"Set out for the great city of Nineveh, and preach against it; their
wickedness has come up before me." But Jonah made ready to flee
to Tarshish away from the LORD. He went down to Joppa, found
a ship going to Tarshish, paid the fare, and went aboard to journey
with them to Tarshish, away from the LORD (Jonah 1:1-3).

The word of the LORD came to Jonah a second time: "Set out for
the great city of Nineveh, and announce to it the message that I
will tell you." So Jonah made ready and went to Nineveh, according to the LORD's bidding. Now Nineveh was an enormously
large city; it took three days to go through it (Jonah 3:1-3).

Jonah's story is too great not to meditate upon, even though
historically it cannot be proven. Like many other Hebrew Scripture stories, it is didactic in form—it is meant to convey a truth
about God in relationship with humanity.

And Jonah is so human. He looks down upon the Ninevites, and this superiority of his leads him away from God. A possible response to a call from God is refusal to cooperate. This is Jonah's choice the first time around in his dialogue with God. He thinks the Ninevites are too low-down to be redeemable. Jonah doesn't even want to go into their neighborhood. Basically he is refusing to love his enemy even when commanded by God. Jonah has a lot of company. Nineveh is the city of Baghdad today. It is a city from which many people think nothing good can come; it is a city with a leader that many think unredeemable.

The issue is not a specific city. It is a mindset that overtakes us when we see objective evil. Fear or disgust leads us to want to flee from the evil and to consider the ones doing the evil as unredeemable, not like us, unworthy of human or divine love. Jonah is easy to relate to—he is like us when we fear our enemy more than we trust God.

God gave Jonah a second chance. God gives us a second, third, fourth, and an infinite number of chances. A key part of allowing ourselves to be used by God in the work of peace is to persevere in the face of our own failures. We may think violent thoughts and do violent actions; we may prejudge and condemn those who frighten or anger us. We may despair of finding a peaceful solution to a long-standing personal or political conflict. To continue to be a person proclaiming God's peace does not mean that we are perfect; however, it does mean that we do not justify the violence that consumes us. Eventually we have to leave the belly of the fish, face God, and acknowledge our sins. God is merciful and patient. Not only will we be forgiven, but we will be used to proclaim the very message of peace from which we ran.

"Ah, LORD GOD!" I said,
  "I know not how to speak; I am too young."
But the LORD answered me,
Say not, "I am too young."
  To whomever I send you, you shall go;
  whatever I command you, you shall speak.

Have no fear before them,
    because I am with you to deliver you,
    says the LORD (Jeremiah 1:6-8).

Jeremiah carried a prejudice within him, a prejudice as to what a prophet of God looked like. Apparently Jeremiah expected God's spokesperson to be older than he. So when God called Jeremiah, he began looking around him to see to whom God was speaking. God couldn't be speaking to Jeremiah! He was too young. God's people are older, wiser.

God allows no room for stereotypes, no time for quibbling about age and readiness. Jeremiah can refuse God, but he can't second-guess God's choice. God knows how old Jeremiah is; he didn't overlook that fact when the call was made. Age has nothing to do with being a proclaimer of God's word. Years later Jesus would gather children around him and remind the adults that a child's heart is necessary for admission to the kingdom of God.[1]

There is an intensity in God's response to Jeremiah's panic. Zeal for the kingdom is pushing Yahweh to send messengers. God can use Jeremiah if he cooperates. Yahweh needs Jeremiah— a concrete instance of the great reality of salvation history being the work of God in cooperation with humanity. Yahweh cannot waste time arguing about Jeremiah's age. It is all God's work. Yahweh reassures Jeremiah that he will be told what to say. He will be protected; there is nothing to fear.

Jeremiah hears God. He embraces the call, knowing that often in his life others will dismiss him as too young or too radical or too morose or too discouraging. God used Jeremiah's hesitant response to teach him a lesson that he would need for all his days. Long after he was no longer young, Jeremiah would feel inadequate and unsure of proclaiming God's message. Few would believe his cries of disaster, because they were living the illusion of security based on power (e.g., Jeremiah 25:3-14; 26:7-24). They had nothing to fear because of their own strength of arms and treaties. Jeremiah was sent to warn them that only in God are

[1] See Matthew 19:13, 14; Mark 10:13-15; Luke 18:15-17.

peace and security. Weapons provide no protection; God alone safeguards the people.

Over and over in his cries to the people, Jeremiah would say, "It is Yahweh who speaks." Jeremiah learned right from the start the source of his words and his strength. Jeremiah was the prophet of Yahweh. He spoke for no other reason, he lived for no one else. All his choices and actions were for the Lord his God. Fidelity from his youth was God's gift to Jeremiah and Jeremiah's gift to God.

You duped me, O LORD, and I let myself be duped;
    you were too strong for me, and you triumphed.
All the day I am an object of laughter;
    everyone mocks me (Jeremiah 20:7).

Words convey emotions. This New American Bible translation uses the word "duped." The Jerusalem Bible uses "seduced," and the New Revised Standard translates it as "enticed." If we consider all the nuances of these words, we get a true sense of the sexual nature of this encounter between Jeremiah and Yahweh. In the first part of this book we considered the scene from God's perspective; now we take it from Jeremiah's. His emotions are conflicted, his sense of his own divine calling tempered by doubts and frustrations.

God is arousing Jeremiah's passions. Signing a deal with God is not exactly the same as a business contract. It is more like a marriage vow. Working with God means being in love with God and the things of God, being consumed by the zeal of God, being on fire with the presence of God. As pressing as Yahweh's love is to Jeremiah, it is Jeremiah's free choice to surrender. Jeremiah wants to give all, but he feels overwhelmed.

Scripture uses strong language. The only way Yahweh can overpower Jeremiah is for Jeremiah to abandon himself to the pulsing desire of Yahweh for him. It is necessary for anyone who is considering entering into a relationship with God to realize how passionate God is. God's love is more powerful than any human force. God desires the individual's personal response, and God desires the spread of the kingdom of God to all people. God is a very demanding lover. No half-hearted responses will be tolerated. Working for Yahweh is a full-time job, no mere Sunday obligation. Jeremiah is not being called to only speak the words of Yahweh; he is being called to be for Yahweh, to exist only for God.

The cry of Jeremiah is, of course, that this same intensity that characterizes his relationship with Yahweh is offered to every person of faith. And nothing less than an equally passionate response can fill the hungering of the human heart and satisfy the yearning of the human spirit. Surrender to Yahweh is the only way to reach full potential in every area of human life.

Do two walk together
   unless they have agreed?
Does a lion roar in the forest
   when it has no prey?
Does a young lion cry out from its den
   unless it has seized something?
Is a bird brought to earth by a snare
   when there is no lure for it?
Does a snare spring up from the ground
   without catching anything?
If the trumpet sounds in a city,
   will the people not be frightened?
If evil befalls a city,
   has not the LORD caused it?
Indeed, the Lord GOD does nothing
   without revealing his plan
   to his servants, the prophets.

The lion roars—
   who will not be afraid!
The Lord GOD speaks—
   who will not prophesy! (Amos 3:3-8).

This is one of those Scripture passages where it is clear who is God and who is not. Yahweh is God, and it is not the role of humans to take God's place. Using nature and animal behavior, the prophet Amos is giving examples of relationships between actions. Two people walk together because they have planned to do so. A lion roars only when threatened; a bird falls when trapped. From the ordinary events of life, Amos reflects on God and humanity. It is a marvelous revelation of God's union with us. Amos claims that God always reveals plans to the people, always brings the people into cooperation with Yahweh. If Yahweh who is God does this, how can anyone refuse to proclaim the message of this God? Amos asks: how anyone can resist the call to prophesy (3:8).

We know that Jonah did; we know that Moses tried to talk God into taking Aaron instead of himself; we know that Jeremiah begged exemption based on his youth. It is a mystery that God chooses us as an act of divine benevolence and yet gives us the freedom to refuse to cooperate.

"Who will not prophesy?" Many can refuse and many do refuse. Even when God sent his Son, many refused to listen and still refuse today. God's love never forces, even though God knows that refusing it brings disaster. Once the experience of God penetrates the human heart, once the love of God is even faintly comprehended, it is almost impossible to refrain from proclaiming the wonders of God. God is speaking to us. Who among us would ever turn from the honor and respect offered by God to throw our lot in with things that lead to destruction and pain? Who among us could turn from the nonviolent peace proclaimed by God to the death-wielding violence proclaimed by society?

A key to understanding Amos's response is to realize how much Amos let the words of Yahweh penetrate his being. Amos could not refuse Yahweh, because he allowed Yahweh to fill his being. To open oneself utterly to God is to risk being filled with the words of Yahweh. Once heard, the message must be shared. As the sound of the trumpet alerts the people in the city, so God's word of unconditional love captures the prophet.

Then spirit lifted me up, and I heard behind me the noise of a loud rumbling as the glory of the LORD rose from its place: the noise made by the wings of the living creatures striking one another, and by the wheels alongside them, a loud rumbling. The spirit which had lifted me up seized me, and I went off spiritually stirred, while the hand of the LORD rested heavily upon me. Thus I came to the exiles who lived at Tel-abib by the river Chebar, and for seven days I sat among them distraught (Ezekiel 3:12-15).

Ezekiel's response to the elaborate visionary call of Yahweh had two key elements. The first is expressed in these early verses. Ezekiel is literally knocked off his feet and swept away by God. He has seen the chariots of God with angels and animals, wings and wheels, fire and light. He recognizes God in the midst of this vision, and he simply can't take it in. Sometimes even a faint reflection of God is too much for a mere mortal to handle. This is definitely one of those times. The Spirit of God intervenes to assist Ezekiel in his response. Ezekiel is lifted up and transported to another place, where he lies in a stupor for seven days.

Ezekiel says that the Lord is resting heavily upon him, and he is distraught. He feels that things are out of his control, and he isn't too thrilled about that fact. This response is as valid and as real as a yes that leads to a leap in faith into the plan of God or a no that leads to a flight away from God. Ezekiel is angry and upset. He is rattled by the spiritual stirring that is going on within him. In this he reveals to us an important step in surrender to God—the step of conversion.

Ezekiel was being called to a vocation so different and mysterious and demanding that he hardly knew himself in the internal shake-up. Dorothy Day, the great American Catholic peace activist, used to say that manual labor is the easiest work, intellectual labor is harder, and spiritual work is the most difficult. It is exhausting business allowing the Spirit to stir our beings to respond to God. For Ezekiel, he needed seven days of rest, seven being a symbolic number referring to perfection. Ezekiel needed time to allow the Spirit to do the work of conversion. Although Ezekiel was angry and confused, he did not refuse. He had the courage to live with the inner confusion that always accompanies a spiritual awakening. The old ways must be let go, and that's the risk: to let oneself be transported to a new place solely by the inspiration of God's Spirit.

The hand of the Lord came upon me, and he said to me: Get up and go out into the plain, where I will speak with you. So I got up and went out into the plain, and I saw that the glory of the LORD was in that place, like the glory I had seen by the river Chebar. I fell prone, but then spirit entered into me and set me on my feet, and he spoke with me (Ezekiel 3:22-24).

Ezekiel has come out of his stupor. He is more at home now with the awesome presence of Yahweh. God asks him to get up and go out to the plain, where God will speak to him. And Ezekiel simply relates, "So I got up and went . . . and saw." An inner conversion has already transformed Ezekiel. He obeys immediately; and in the act of obedience is recognition of the glory of God.

We never lose by being obedient to God. If we go wherever God is moving us, interiorly or exteriorly, we will see the glory of God as Ezekiel did. It need not be a vision or a physical presence, but it will be as real. Following God's call gives an inner conviction that is stronger than even doubt and spiritual darkness. In the beginning God leads us with signs and inner visions. As the faith journey continues, the emotional feeling of following God slips away. We are left with nothing but faith. In time this becomes a greater gift than all the signs we ever had.

Ezekiel is on the journey toward becoming a spokesperson for God. He follows of his own accord. Now he prostrates himself in worship of God without being in a stupor. He expresses with his prone body the total surrender of his heart to the all-powerful God. The Spirit enters him and gives him the strength to stand and speaks to him. God accepts worship, rejoices in seeing us give praise. But God wants us to get about the business of being kingdom-seekers. God nudges us upright to embrace the call to listen to the Spirit and then to speak the message of peace to all people. Part of the experience of praising God is to proclaim the glory of God to all people by the way we live. Surrender to God always leads to commitment to the work of God.

The Babylonians had an idol called Bel, and every day they provided for it six barrels of fine flour, forty sheep, and six measures of wine. The king worshiped it and went every day to adore it; but Daniel adored only his God. When the king asked him, "Why do you not adore Bel?" Daniel replied, "Because I worship not idols made with hands, but only the living God who made heaven and earth and has dominion over all mankind." . . . There was a great dragon which the Babylonians worshiped. "Look!" said the king to Daniel, "you cannot deny that this is a living god, so adore it." But Daniel answered, "I adore the Lord, my God, for he is the living God (Daniel 14:3-5, 23-25).

Although this book fits more in the category of apocalyptic and Daniel is not considered a major prophet, he gives us an amazing insight into being faithful to God in everyday business life. Daniel was an advisor to a series of kings, Nebuchadnezzar being the most famous. He assisted the king in interpretation of dreams and in settling disputes. Probably his most famous day in court was the one on which he represented the innocent Susanna and saved her from false accusations (Daniel 13).

Daniel seemed to be able to balance service to the king with worship of his God. This is the aspect of Daniel that is worth considering for reflection on being a spokesperson for God in the fray of daily life. Daniel shows on several specific occasions that when the things of God are in conflict with the things of the king, there is no choice. God alone is to be served. The king is only obeyed when he is not in conflict with God's laws.

Daniel is faithful from the beginning when it involves the dietary laws of the Hebrews, and he is faithful as he rises in influence in the king's court. His response to any request from the king is always measured against his fidelity to God. So when the king asks Daniel to worship the idol called Bel or the other idol that is a dragon, Daniel does not hesitate to refuse. He clearly states his loyalty, "I worship the Lord my God." Daniel responds to tests against his faith regardless of the cost. He is fearless in the face of apparent state power.

Time and again Daniel gets sent to hungry lions (Daniel 6). Through the grace of God, the lions remain hungry and Daniel is never harmed. To Daniel life or death is immaterial as long as he lives or dies worshiping his Lord. Daniel's lifelong response to the Lord's love is fidelity.

Thus says the LORD regarding the prophets
    who lead my people astray;
Who, when their teeth have something to bite,
    announce peace,
But when one fails to put something in their mouth,
    proclaim war against him.
Therefore you shall have night, not vision,
    darkness, not divination;
The sun shall go down upon the prophets,
    and the day shall be dark for them.
Then shall the seers be put to shame,
    and the diviners confounded;
They shall cover their lips, all of them,
    because there is no answer from God.
But as for me, I am filled with power,
    with the spirit of the LORD,
    with authority and with might;
To declare to Jacob his crimes
    and to Israel his sins (Micah 3:5-8).

The Scripture brings us into Micah's story midstream. We don't have the initial call from God and the response from Micah. What we do have are the passionate words of a prophet who is committed to preaching the message of Yahweh regardless of the reaction he will encounter. Micah clearly acknowledges the truth that people are swayed politically toward whoever is satisfying their needs. If they have what they need, they are happy; if not, they are unsettled and disruptive.

In times of economic growth most don't care what the politicians do as long as life is good. In bad times the condemnation of authority accompanies economic hardships. And those in the worst predicament are those who tell people things they don't want to hear.

Micah pushes ahead full steam. His popularity is of no concern to him. He is about God's business, and the apparent success or failure of his preaching is irrelevant. The only thing that matters is that Micah be faithful to Yahweh. Micah knows that some false prophets hesitate to give the tough demands of Yahweh because they will not be loved for doing so. Micah is exuberant in his confidence. "But as for me, I am filled with power, / with the spirit of the LORD, / with authority and with might" (3:8). Micah's response to Yahweh is to embrace joyfully the word of Yahweh no matter how difficult and to trust completely in God's word. The people of Judah did not want to hear Micah proclaim God's cry for repentance and renewal, for a return to justice and tenderness. Micah preached it anyway.

God's ways are not always popular, and to preach them often pits the prophet against the tidal wave of culture. In a society accustomed to resolving conflicts with violence, the ways of peace seem naive and ineffectual. The prophets of peace are dismissed as well-intentioned, misinformed idealists lacking a sense of reality. As Micah proclaimed without fear God's ways to his people, declaring "to Jacob his crimes and to Israel his sins" (3:8), so also are today's prophets called to proclaim the ways of God to a world consumed by power. They may have to speak in the face of derision and ridicule. Their strength comes from the Spirit of God, the breath of God within them. It is God's word of peace that must be spoken fearlessly, however challenging it may be. After all, we are full of the strength of God, and God's power will endure forever.

So I will allure her;
I will lead her into the desert
and speak to her heart.
From there I will give her the vineyards she had,
and the valley of Achor as a door of hope.
She shall respond there as in the days of her youth,
when she came up from the land of Egypt.

On that day, says the LORD,
She shall call me "My husband,"
and never again "My baal."

> Then will I remove from her mouth the names of the Baals,
> so that they shall no longer be invoked.
> I will make a covenant for them on that day,
> with the beasts of the field,
> With the birds of the air,
> and with the things that crawl on the ground.
> Bow and sword and war
> I will destroy from the land,
> and I will let them take their rest in security.
>
> I will espouse you to me forever:
> I will espouse you in right and in justice,
> in love and in mercy;
> I will espouse you in fidelity,
> and you shall know the LORD.
> On that day I will respond, says the LORD;
> I will respond to the heavens,
> and they shall respond to the earth;
> The earth shall respond to the grain, and wine, and oil,
> and these shall respond to Jezreel.
> I will sow him for myself in the land,
> and I will have pity on Lo-ruhama.
> I will say to Lo-ammi, "You are my people,"
> and he shall say, "My God!" (Hosea 2:16-25).

The names of Hosea's children are important in under-standing this passage. "Lo-ruhamah" means "Not pitied," and "Lo-ammi" means "Not my people." We consider in this passage the response of Yahweh to someone who has been unfaithful to God. This response gives us insight into the perseverance of God for union with us. God never just calls us, waits for a response, and then forgets about us. God calls over and over; and it seems as if nothing keeps God from continually pursuing us. God takes us who are not pitied and gives us pity, and he takes as his own those of us who are not his people.

God cannot leave us alone. God loves us and tells us, "You are my people." The example of God in Hosea prepares the prophet of peace for dealing with rejection. God teaches us by his own example: as God never gives up, so we can never stop trying to reach out to those who bitterly oppose us or the ways of peace. Right, justice, love, and mercy are the characteristics of espousal with God. We are called to be the same with others as God is with us.

In Hosea, Yahweh always loves, even through the gross infidelity of the spouse. In other words, God always acts as a loving God despite an unloving response. Part of responding to God as a prophet of peace is being faithful to the message in circumstances where we don't feel peaceful or loving. Responding to God's call to be a proclaimer of peace is to be willing to do so against personal feelings of anger or revenge. God calls us to respond to our call in good times and in bad times with mercy and justice to all. Until we can look with love on all the "Unloved" ones among us, we cannot live in an abiding position of peace. Hosea teaches us that response is not a unique, one-time only experience but an enduring way of living in the loving ways of God.

The oracle which Habakkuk the prophet received in vision.

How long, O LORD? I cry for help
    but you do not listen!
I cry out to you, "Violence!"
    but you do not intervene.
Why do you let me see ruin;
    why must I look at misery?
Destruction and violence are before me;
    there is strife, and clamorous discord.
This is why the law is benumbed,
    and judgment is never rendered:
Because the wicked circumvent the just;
    this is why judgment comes forth perverted.

I will stand at my guard post,
    and station myself upon the rampart,
And keep watch to see what he will say to me,
    and what answer he will give to my complaint.

Then the LORD answered me and said:
    Write down the vision

Clearly upon the tablets,
    so that one can read it readily.
For the vision still has its time,
    presses on to fulfillment, and will not disappoint;
If it delays, wait for it,
    it will surely come, it will not be late (Habakkuk 1:1-4; 2:1-3).

Habakkuk is alive at the same time as Jeremiah, so things aren't going well for God's chosen people. Enemies are within and without. Foreign powers threaten their very existence, and infidelity eats away at their relationship with God, their only hope. The Babylonians are about to attack; the fall of Jerusalem is imminent. Habakkuk is called to dialogue with God about these horrible events.

It is true that the Israelites have been bad, but does that mean that they should be destroyed by even worse people? Habakkuk introduces a challenge to the ways of God by a human being. Habakkuk is asking two questions of God: "Where are you?" and "Why me?" We all ask these at some point in our lives, and often many times. Habakkuk is asking on behalf of all the people. It is as if he is demanding an accountability from God for allowing bad things to happen to his people.

What is crucial in this story is what Habakkuk does after he asks the questions. He goes up to the sentry post and waits for God to answer. Here is the distinction between whining and dialogue. All of us can gripe and feel sorry for ourselves and shift the blame to other people and events. The prophet is showing what a person of faith does at a crisis moment in life. In fear and panic the cry to God is made, even questioning God's apparent indifference to evil. But the great revelation through Habakkuk is that the person of faith trusts, even in dire situations, and waits for the response of God.

God will later answer Habakkuk and reveal that much of what is happening to the Israelites is the result of their own faithless corruption. But the response of the people, even while enduring the consequences of their own sins, must always be to wait in hope and trust and love of Yahweh. Evil actions lead to dire results, but God is faithful and will never abandon the people. The faithful one waits, for the vision will come, however slowly.

Then Zechariah said to the angel, "How shall I know this? For I am an old man, and my wife is advanced in years." And the angel said to him in reply, "I am Gabriel, who stand before God. I was sent to speak to you and to announce to you this good news. But now you will be speechless and unable to talk until the day these things take place, because you did not believe my words, which will be fulfilled at their proper time" (Luke 1:18-20).

Zechariah's response to the call of God came in two phases. This is the first, the skeptical one. Zechariah isn't convinced that the angel is believable, because the message seems impossible. That's the crux of the problem for Zechariah—the realm of possibility of what God asks. For anyone trying to live the gospel, the possible is always the stumbling block for the holy.

Zechariah is a great help to us because of his very fear of God's ways. His weak-hearted response is matched by the certitude of Gabriel's. If we stand in God's presence, as Gabriel does continually, then the ways of God, however impossible they may appear, are embraced and lived enthusiastically. Zechariah needed faith to respond to God, because God was calling him beyond the limitations of human reality. Zechariah wavered. Fear was his response to God.

Sometimes we respond in the same way. We claim efficiency or practicality as excuses for not living the radical gospel of Jesus Christ. Gabriel is setting straight all of us as well as Zechariah: "I was sent to speak to you and to announce to you this good news" (Luke 1:19). God is God, and the only proper response to God is boundless faith and complete trust. But when we fall short of these, it is reassuring to know that God accepts even a hint of good will on our part and uses it to do great things. Zechariah lacked a full faith in his response, yet God still used him to bring about the good news.

When they came on the eighth day to circumcise the child, they were going to call him Zechariah after his father, but his mother said in reply, "No. He will be called John." But they answered her, "There is no one among your relatives who has this name." So they made signs, asking his father what he wished him to be called. He asked for a tablet and wrote, "John is his name," and all were amazed. Immediately his mouth was opened, his tongue freed, and he spoke blessing God.

"Blessed be the Lord, the God of Israel,
     for he has visited and brought redemption to his people.
He has raised up a horn for our salvation
     within the house of David his servant,
even as he promised through the mouth of his holy
          prophets from of old:
          salvation from our enemies and from the hand
          of all who hate us,
     to show mercy to our fathers
     and to be mindful of his holy covenant
and of the oath he swore to Abraham our father,
     and to grant us that,
rescued from the hand of enemies,
     without fear we might worship him
in holiness and righteousness
     before him all our days.
And you, child, will be called prophet of the Most High,
     for you will go before the Lord to prepare his ways,
to give his people knowledge of salvation
     through the forgiveness of their sins,
     because of the tender mercy of our God
     by which the daybreak from on high will visit us
to shine on those who sit in darkness and death's shadow,
     to guide our feet into the path of peace" (Luke 1:59-64, 68-79).

Here is Zechariah in the second phase of his response to God. The nine months of silence and watching his child grow in Elizabeth have produced a more faithful person. In our world of high technology and multisensory imaging, silence and watchfulness are rare commodities. In general, society today seems impatient to a fault. This is the age of road rage and riots, of child abuse and domestic assaults. We seem unable to give each other any leeway. Even so-called peacemakers violently condemn those they see as being unjust or oppressive. Many a war or personal conflict has escalated when one party assumes the stance of self-righteousness.

Justice demands that we speak the truth, but justice also demands that we listen and wait for God to move us. The work of peace is not merely the human response to the violence in society. The work of peace is the person of Jesus present in us in every aspect of human life. To be Christ we must spend our days listening to him and waiting until he moves within us. Injustice is not our motivation; the good news of Jesus Christ is. We will still work against injustice, but it will be because it is not the way of God, not just because we think it is wrong. There is a world of difference between these two motivations.

With one we are dependent upon our own judgment and good will, which will fail all of us at some time or another. With the second motivation, that of being Christ, we are simply servants of his, dedicated to his message and his ways of proclaiming it. Silence and watchfulness precede and accompany any action for peace, so that we can be attentive to the word of God growing within us.

When the time for speech comes, as it did for Zechariah, our mouths will proclaim the peace of God. Praise is the appropriate response to God's call. Lives of justice and truth are lives of praise. Zechariah blessed God for all the wonders God was doing. Zechariah proclaimed the light that would destroy the darkness and the mercy of God that would lead everyone in the ways of peace. Every action for peace is meant to be a proclamation of God's light in the darkness. Every peacemaker is an announcer of the light of Christ in the dark world of violence.

Mary said, "Behold, I am the handmaid of the Lord. May it be done to me according to your word." Then the angel departed from her (Luke 1:38).

Of all the words spoken by human beings throughout history, none are as passionate and powerful as these. Mary teaches us the perfect response to the call of God—total surrender. Mary has been asked to so something so far beyond the realm of human possibility that it cannot even be believed without faith. She is asked to be the mother of God. She is asked to allow the child to be conceived in her by the Holy Spirit without human intercourse. She is asked to assume the role of unwed mother in a society that stoned women in that situation.

Unlike many other prophets, Mary offers no resistance. She neither balks at the impossible nor runs from the consequences. She does ask the angel for clarity. Will the child be conceived by means other than human? When the angel reveals the role of the Holy Spirit, Mary abandons herself fully and completely to her God. This is not the response of a naive girl. It is the response of a young woman confident in her God. Mary is so in love with Yahweh that she has no fear. There are no gritted teeth and anxious heart palpitations. This is the moment of union. Mary knows God and God knows Mary. Their love takes flesh in the child in her womb.

Every one of us is called to the same vocation: to bear Christ in our time and in our place. Like Mary, we are to do this by confident love. Surrender in love is the most mature response an adult can make to anyone. To make it to God is to be most fully alive. Mary's abandonment is Mary's response, and this is her greatness. Our own greatness, like Mary's, is not in what we accomplish but in what we allow God to accomplish in us.

———————

Now this is how the birth of Jesus Christ came about. When his mother Mary was betrothed to Joseph, but before they lived together, she was found with child through the holy Spirit. Joseph her husband, since he was a righteous man, yet unwilling to expose her to shame, decided to divorce her quietly. Such was his intention when, behold, the angel of the Lord appeared to him in a dream and said, "Joseph, son of David, do not be afraid to take Mary your wife into your home. For it is through the holy Spirit that this child has been conceived in her. She will bear a son and you are to name him Jesus, because he will save his people from their sins." All this took place to fulfill what the Lord had said through the prophet:

"Behold, the virgin shall be with child and bear a son,
    and they shall name him Emmanuel,"

which means "God is with us." When Joseph awoke, he did as the angel of the Lord had commanded him and took his wife into his home. He had no relations with her until she bore a son, and he named him Jesus (Matthew 1:18-25).

Devotions to Saint Joseph abound in the Church. He is one popular man among the saints of God. Yet the Gospel tells so little of the story of Joseph. We know that he and Mary were in love, engaged to be married. We know through this story and the presentation in the Temple that he observed the law. He was of the house of David and chosen to be stepfather to Jesus. The Gospel calls Joseph a just man, the highest compliment for a Hebrew.

For now, let us look at Joseph as prophet. Joseph is called by God to love Mary. That part is probably easy. They fall in love and plan to marry. God intervenes in an extraordinary way, impregnating Mary by the power of the Holy Spirit and leaving Joseph in the dark at first. Joseph neither condemns nor abandons the woman he loves. He and Mary are betrothed. At that time in the Hebrew culture, betrothal was a legal but not a sexual union, which is why Joseph's plans can be seen as a protection of Mary. He prepares to make arrangements required by law to keep Mary's name and person safe. God again intervenes—this time with Joseph, informing him of the father of the child and asking his cooperation in the birth of Jesus.

Angels and dreams aside, this has to be overwhelming for Joseph to absorb except in faith. Joseph faces a crisis in his faith. He is already living a dutiful life with God. He is religious and just, following the precepts of God as set down through the law and the prophets. But God disrupts even a good life for a greater one. It is easy to understand God calling someone from sin to life, but it is harder to see God calling a faithful person into crisis. Something in us wants to cry out to God, "Aren't you ever satisfied?" History, especially salvation history as recorded in the Scriptures, gives the answer: No. God's love is beyond all our good intentions and sincere efforts, so God will always call us beyond our human limitations to greater and greater love. As long as we have breath in our bodies, we are never at perfect love. No matter how many times we have responded to God in the past, there will always be another call, another angel, another dream.

Joseph gives us an example of a faithful response to a very disturbing call. Joseph obeys in utter simplicity and complete faithfulness. His response is immediate and total. He will take Mary in a way he never expected. He will claim Jesus as his own by naming him. And he will assume the role of father to the Son of God on this earth. This will take him to Bethlehem, Egypt, and then back to Nazareth—all the details in obedience to the will of God.

When the angels went away from them to heaven, the shepherds said to one another, "Let us go, then, to Bethlehem to see this thing that has taken place, which the Lord has made known to us." So they went in haste and found Mary and Joseph, and the infant lying in the manger. When they saw this, they made known the message that had been told them about this child. All who heard it were amazed by what had been told them by the shepherds. And Mary kept all these things, reflecting on them in her heart. Then the shepherds returned, glorifying and praising God for all they had heard and seen, just as it had been told to them (Luke 2:15-20).

Elaborate crèches display the shepherds in a beautiful pastoral scene. Their clothes are simple but adequate, their faces radiant, and their sheep white and fluffy. In reality shepherds smell and the sheep are dirty. In Jesus' day shepherds were the outcasts of society. And it was to such as these that the angels came. Rugged individuals used to survival on the edge, the shepherds heard what kings and rabbis refused to hear: Jesus Christ, the Savior of the world, was born of a woman.

The shepherds went to Bethlehem. Surely these men did not comprehend all that was going on. Their lives didn't allow them long hours of study and prayer in the synagogue to enable them to recognize all the signs of the Messiah. Simple laborers, rough people, illiterate men, they accepted the angels' message and heeded it in the way they were capable of—they walked to Bethlehem with their sheep.

When God calls us, he does not expect us to become different people in our response. God calls us in our uniqueness and desires our response in the same uniqueness. Unlike these trusting shepherds, we often waste time and energy on our unworthiness. None of us is perfect; and God does not expect us to be that. As we journey in God's way we learn and grow, but we always are fully accepted by God, no matter our condition or position in life. Each of us is created in the image and likeness of God; each of us is called to follow our Creator and Savior God just as we are, not as we wish we were. Self-acceptance is one of the prerequisites for a full response to God's loving call.

When we are comfortable with ourselves, we are capable of moving out to others, even to God. The shepherds received the angels' presence and message and moved. They were not called directly by Jesus, for he was still an infant. But their call is similar to the ones Jesus himself would make in his lifetime. Jesus would do as the angels did: announce by his presence the kingdom of God and then invite. Blessed are those who accept the invitation and go to see the newborn baby.

Once in the presence of Christ, the shepherds became disciples proclaiming, praising, and glorifying God. God accepts our steps toward Christ and sets us on the path of discipleship. Response is a process of listening and proclaiming, a union of God's work and ours, a journey of discovery with God and of God.

When Jesus was born in Bethlehem of Judea, in the days of King Herod, behold, magi from the east arrived in Jerusalem, saying, "Where is the newborn king of the Jews? We saw his star at its rising and have come to do him homage." When King Herod heard this, he was greatly troubled, and all Jerusalem with him. . . .

Then Herod called the magi secretly and ascertained from them the time of the star's appearance. He sent them to Bethlehem and said, "Go and search diligently for the child. When you have found him, bring me word, that I too may go and do him homage." After their audience with the king they set out. And behold, the star that they had seen at its rising preceded them, until it came and stopped over the place where the child was. They were overjoyed at seeing the star, and on entering the house they saw the child with Mary his mother. They prostrated themselves and did him homage. Then they opened their treasures and offered him gifts of gold, frankincense, and myrrh. And having been warned in a dream not to return to Herod, they departed for their country by another way (Matthew 2:1-3, 7-12).

Both Herod and the Magi received notice of the birth of the Messiah. The Magi were called through the stars, which they were trained to observe. Herod was originally informed by them and then consulted his chief priests and scribes for further clarification and verification of the facts.

This Christmas story reveals two possible responses to a call from God, positive and negative. The Magi, the outsiders, the foreigners, followed, saw and believed. Herod, the local boy, turned his back on God's call and responded with murderous hatred.[2] The Scriptures reveal nothing of Herod's motives, only his actions, so we don't know why he was so threatened by the birth of the Messiah. A safe guess might be that the powerful are always left insecure in the presence of someone over whom they have neither authority nor power.

The Magi traveled to a foreign country and recognized and worshiped the God of strangers. A call from God goes beyond the human experience and can bring someone into a new reality. The Magi ventured into this new place and were rewarded with the living God. Part of their response was to alter their habits and customs. They would have to return to their own country by another way. Response to God calls for change. Things cannot always remain the same when God enters into the picture. Practices and procedures now are measured according to God's ways, not our own, so often some familiar territory is left behind. A new way for a new response. We lay our gifts before God, and then we go in whatever direction the Lord indicates through his messengers. The details are important, and in them we enflesh our heart's response to a call of love.

---

[2] For a more detailed analysis of this story, see Raymond Brown, *An Adult Christ at Christmas* (Collegeville, Minn.: The Liturgical Press, 1979).

Then Jesus came from Galilee to John at the Jordan to be baptized by him. John tried to prevent him, saying, "I need to be baptized by you, and yet you are coming to me?" Jesus said to him in reply, "Allow it now, for thus it is fitting for us to fulfill all righteousness." Then he allowed him (Matthew 3:13-15).

So they [John's disciples] came to John and said to him, "Rabbi, the one who was with you across the Jordan, to whom you testified, here he is baptizing and everyone is coming to him." John answered and said, "No one can receive anything except what has been given him from heaven. You yourselves can testify that I said [that] I am not the Messiah, but that I was sent before him. The one who has the bride is the bridegroom; the best man, who stands and listens to him, rejoices greatly at the bridegroom's voice. So this joy of mine has been made complete. He must increase; I must decrease."

The one who comes from above is above all (John 3:26-31).

John the Baptist's response to Christ is a combination of obedience and humility. John recognizes Jesus by the Jordan River, where John is on mission. He attempts to introduce Jesus as Messiah to the people gathered there. Jesus alters John's plans and takes a turn with him that John never expected: Jesus asks John to baptize him. John is really thrown by this; it was probably the last thing that he expected Jesus to ask. John knows that Jesus is the Holy One who needs no baptism, but Jesus has yet to reveal to the world his solidarity with sinners. This is the initial revelation of that reality. Jesus takes on our sinful nature when he steps into the Jordan for baptism. John, not understanding any of this, cooperates.

When we know something is from God, we are called to obey even before understanding is given us. This kind of response is one of pure faith. There is no seduction or consolation, just the request "Will you do this for me?" John does what Jesus asks of him. It is that simple and that necessary. Obedience to the will of God is the primary response of a disciple.

The second story involving John gives an insight into John's unhesitating obedience. John was a humble man. He knew that he was not God; his role in life was to prepare the way for Christ. True humility is not self-abasement but joy in one's self. John had a clear sense of his vocation: to point out the person of Christ to a prepared people. John's ego was in tune with his being a precursor of the Lord. He was responding to Christ for Christ's sake, not for his own ambition and satisfaction. With all our mixed motivations and suffocating personal needs, the bottom line of response to God is that it is for God's glory and not our own.

The joy John expressed awaits us when we focus our attention on the bridegroom's presence. It is easy to fall into the trap that advancement in the spiritual life carries honor and prestige with it. On the contrary, spiritual growth leads to the prominence of God, not self. Humility, being at one with our place in the grand scheme of God's creation, must accompany the desire to follow Christ. Humility is the foundation of obedience, which is the core of response to God's call.

> As he was walking by the Sea of Galilee, he saw two brothers, Simon who is called Peter, and his brother Andrew, casting a net into the sea; they were fishermen. He said to them, "Come after me, and I will make you fishers of men." At once they left their nets and followed him. He walked along from there and saw two other brothers, James, the son of Zebedee, and his brother John. They were in a boat, with their father Zebedee, mending their nets. He called them, and immediately they left their boat and their father and followed him (Matthew 4:18-22).
>
> As Jesus passed on from there, he saw a man named Matthew sitting at the customs post. He said to him, "Follow me." And he got up and followed him (Matthew 9:9).

Peter, James, John, and Matthew made mistakes in their path to discipleship. The Gospel doesn't hide their weaknesses or their sins. But in these passages we see their initial wholehearted response to their Lord. They heard Jesus call them, and they left everything—boats, fathers, fishing nets, careers. They followed Jesus immediately. The Scriptures say "at once." The person of Jesus is compassionate and forgiving, but he is also demanding. He is God and, as God, asks for our whole heart, our whole soul, and our whole being. There can be no measured response to God's call. God does not ask for a piece of us on a Sunday morning or a token act of mercy in a soup kitchen or shelter. God does not expect us to share only our old clothes with the poor. Jesus demands a torrent of love. He wants us to give the clothes off our backs, to take the poor into our homes, to serve our own soup and bread. Jesus' love calls for a response in kind. He gave himself completely to the Father for love of the Father and the love of us. Therefore, to be a disciple of this Jesus is to give ourselves totally and completely to the Father for the love of the Father, the love of Jesus, and the love of all Jesus' brothers and sisters.

The nets and fishing boats and tax collector's table may not look like much in worldly possessions. They were the livelihood of Peter, James, John, and Matthew. They were all they had known in their lives and would most probably be all they would ever know. Career options were limited in those days. And these young men gave it all up to follow their Lord. No less is expected of us today. Nothing is ours—all is God's.

Now someone approached him and said, "Teacher, what good must I do to gain eternal life?" He answered him, "Why do you ask me about the good? There is only One who is good. If you wish to enter into life, keep the commandments." He asked him, "Which ones?" And Jesus replied, "'You shall not kill; you shall not commit adultery; you shall not steal; you shall not bear false witness; honor your father and your mother'; and 'you shall love your neighbor as yourself.'" The young man said to him, "All of these I have observed. What do I still lack?" Jesus said to him, "If you wish to be perfect, go, sell what you have and give to [the] poor, and you will have treasure in heaven. Then come, follow me." When the young man heard this statement, he went away sad, for he had many possessions (Matthew 19:16-22).

Both Jesus and the young man left this encounter saddened.[3] The call was out there. The young man's initial attraction

---

[3] For more reflection on this story, see Patricia McCarthy, C.N.D., *Of Passion and Folly* (Collegeville, Minn.: The Liturgical Press, 1996).

to Jesus brought him into conversation with the Son of God. Jesus must have seen the spark of desire in a young heart weighed down by possessions yet straining to be free. Jesus loved him and tried to free him. Even though Jesus knew what would make this young person happy, he did not force it on him. Jesus offered and left himself vulnerable to be rejected.

Response to God must always be free. Only a free heart can praise, only a free spirit can worship, only a free person can surrender. We are held back from freedom by our own choices. Failure to extricate ourselves from our possessions or worries or ambitions can cause the flame of surrender to flicker weakly and eventually die out. If we wonder why God isn't using us or speaking to us, in honesty we must look to see what material or spiritual possessions are blocking our ears and hearts.

St. John of the Cross used to say that a small string can keep a bird from flying as well as a strong chain. Part of responding to God is to work at freeing ourselves from the ties that bind. It is a lifetime of work. This young man in the Gospel did not face his crisis of possessions versus life only this one time. Many times in his life he would have had to deal with it. Perhaps at another time the draw of freedom would have outweighed the lure of money and he might have chosen differently. We only know this part of the story.

In our own lives, the more we give ourselves to the materialism of the day, the less we hear the word of God calling with a promise of real freedom and joy. All our efforts to divest ourselves of money and possessions till the soil of discipleship. In time the flower will grow if the seed has been nourished. God's call is pure gift, which we never earn or deserve; but our own efforts to be free of other attachments open our beings to receive the proffered gift. "God does not fit in an occupied heart."[4]

Now when Jesus was in Bethany in the house of Simon the leper, a woman came up to him with an alabaster jar of costly perfumed

---

[4] St. John of the Cross, *The Living Flame of Love: Versions A and B,* trans. Jane Ackerman (Binghamton, N.Y.: Medieval & Renaissance Texts & Studies, 1995).

oil, and poured it on his head while he was reclining at table. When the disciples saw this, they were indignant and said, "Why this waste? It could have been sold for much, and the money given to the poor." Since Jesus knew this, he said to them, "Why do you make trouble for the woman? She has done a good thing for me. The poor you will always have with you; but you will not always have me. In pouring this perfumed oil upon my body, she did it to prepare me for burial. Amen, I say to you, wherever this gospel is proclaimed in the whole world, what she has done will be spoken of, in memory of her" (Matthew 26:6-13).

A Pharisee invited him to dine with him, and he entered the Pharisee's house and reclined at table. Now there was a sinful woman in the city who learned that he was at table in the house of the Pharisee. Bringing an alabaster flask of ointment, she stood behind him at his feet weeping and began to bathe his feet with her tears. Then she wiped them with her hair, kissed them, and anointed them with the ointment. When the Pharisee who had invited him saw this he said to himself, "If this man were a prophet, he would know who and what sort of woman this is who is touching him, that she is a sinner." . . . Then he turned to the woman and said to Simon, "Do you see this woman? When I entered your house, you did not give me water for my feet, but she has bathed them with her tears and wiped them with her hair. You did not give me a kiss, but she has not ceased kissing my feet since the time I entered. You did not anoint my head with oil, but she anointed my feet with ointment. So I tell you, her many sins have been forgiven; hence, she has shown great love. But the one to whom little is forgiven, loves little." He said to her, "Your sins are forgiven." The others at table said to themselves, "Who is this who even forgives sins?" But he said to the woman, "Your faith has saved you; go in peace" (Luke 7:36-39, 44-50).

There is no consensus among Scripture scholars concerning certain details in these two stories. They may have been both about the same woman, or they may have been two separate women. For our reflection either version fits. These stories dramatically portray the response of passionate love to Jesus. Both express women understanding the need of the human heart to go to extremes for the Beloved. One of these women may have been

Mary, sister of Lazarus, a respected woman from a respected family. The other could have been a sinner, scorned publicly, shunned by the respectable people of the town. The anointing of the head is associated with burial and kingship, the anointing of the feet with repentance for sin.

Both women were called and welcomed by Jesus. In his presence both women responded with pure hearts. Love cannot contain itself; it must pour itself out in action. Both women took the radical, extravagant approach to their Lord. Using expensive perfume, they anointed their Lord. He deserved the best; they needed to pour the best over him. They were seduced by a passionate God and responded in kind. Braving the scorn of the self-righteous, politically correct men who were ignoring their Beloved, they entered into places where they weren't welcome. They worshiped and loved their Lord publicly, passionately, and unashamedly. Their love was their courage and their fearlessness.

In both these stories we see not only the response of loving disciples but the response of Jesus to those who follow. Jesus appreciated and supported these women, defending them to those who criticized their actions. He was touched in body with their perfume and in being with their love. Christ will always respond to our own responses. As abandoned as we are, he will be more so.

When we follow Christ, there will be legions of people to condemn and criticize us; but it does not matter. What others say about us or do to us is irrelevant. Only the love of the lover matters. "It is only the love of the lover which penetrates the heart of God."[5] Jesus accepts our perfume and rejoices in our abandonment. He sends us forth forgiven, loved, peaceful and on fire with his own burning love.

Philip found Nathanael and told him, "We have found the one about whom Moses wrote in the law, and also the prophets, Jesus, son of Joseph, from Nazareth." But Nathanael said to him, "Can anything good come from Nazareth?" Philip said to him, "Come

[5] *The Writings of Marguerite Bourgeoys,* Congregation of Notre Dame, (Montreal, 1976) 58.

and see." Jesus saw Nathanael coming toward him and said of him, "Here is a true Israelite. There is no duplicity in him." Nathanael said to him, "How do you know me?" Jesus answered and said to him, "Before Philip called you, I saw you under the fig tree." Nathanael answered him, "Rabbi, you are the Son of God; you are the King of Israel." Jesus answered and said to him, "Do you believe because I told you that I saw you under the fig tree? You will see greater things than this" (John 1:45-50).

Nathanael was a skeptic and a bit snobbish, at least with regard to those folks who hailed from Nazareth. When the call of Jesus came to him through his friend Philip, Nathanael didn't buy in at first. But neither did he dismiss Philip's suggestion outright. This is another wonderful example of the humanity of the apostles. This is the "nudge" version of God calling us.

Sometimes we get a little poke from God—not exactly the beatific vision, just a push in a direction we might not be heading. We have a ton of work to do, and someone calls who needs us immediately. A friend cajoles us into helping out at a soup kitchen. A young woman needs a safe place to stay away from an abusive husband. Prayers for career opportunities are answered in ways we never dreamed—not our first choice! All these experiences and situations are the realities that may be pointing to a call from God.

Nathanael is a great example to follow. Despite his initial reluctance, he goes to see; he gives God a chance to enter. He is open to a new experience, a new encounter with the Almighty. He responds not with enthusiasm but with vulnerability. Christ, who knows what is in the human heart (John 2:25), welcomes Nathanael and acknowledges his purity of heart. Then Christ, responding to Nathanael's hesitant steps, reveals something personal known only to Nathanael and Jesus. He enters into immediate intimacy. And Nathanael is hooked. Skepticism and reluctance have become intimacy and surrender.

Weak, feeble-hearted response to God can become, by the awesome grace of God, wholehearted abandonment. God is waiting to capture our hearts, but there has to be that first initial movement of our own toward the Christ, the Son of the living

God. Without our response Christ cannot bring us further into his heart and mission.

———————

> Then Jesus came with them to a place called Gethsemane, and he said to his disciples, "Sit here while I go over there and pray." He took along Peter and the two sons of Zebedee, and began to feel sorrow and distress. Then he said to them, "My soul is sorrowful even to death. Remain here and keep watch with me." He advanced a little and fell prostrate in prayer, saying, "My Father, if it is possible, let this cup pass from me; yet, not as I will, but as you will." When he returned to his disciples he found them asleep. He said to Peter, "So you could not keep watch with me for one hour? Watch and pray that you may not undergo the test. The spirit is willing, but the flesh is weak." Withdrawing a second time, he prayed again, "My Father, if it is not possible that this cup pass without my drinking it, your will be done!" Then he returned once more and found them asleep, for they could not keep their eyes open. He left them and withdrew again and prayed a third time, saying the same thing again. Then he returned to his disciples and said to them, "Are you still sleeping and taking your rest? Behold, the hour is at hand when the Son of Man is to be handed over to sinners. Get up, let us go. Look, my betrayer is at hand" (Matthew 26:36-46).

Prayer—honest, persevering, desperate prayer—is often the only response we can make to God. But we will not be able to pray in times of trial if we have not prayed day after day in every situation and every predicament. Jesus prayed always. Scripture records a handful of times he left the crowds and the disciples to spend time alone with his Father. Jesus is God and he needed the time. In these last days of his life Jesus seems unable to convey the message of the necessity of prayer to his disciples. Even his special friends, Peter, James, and John, fail him in his time of need; they aren't ready and attentive to the signs from God. Distractions and fatigue override Christ's plea for companionship.

Jesus alone prays the prayer of the committed lover. Jesus is in anguish, knowing what he is about to face. He is fully human and fully frightened because of that. Terror has gripped his being.

In agony and sweat he pours out his heart and fears to a God who seems distant even to his only Son. Jesus perseveres. He continues in the same response he has made his entire life on earth. He surrenders to the will of God. In the Temple at age twelve, his reason for staying was his Father's business (Luke 2:41-49). At his baptism by John his motivation was the Father's desire (Matthew 3:13-17). His mission on earth was to praise and honor the Father, to make the Father's name known to all people.

Now, at a time when Jesus is experiencing overwhelming fear in anticipation of betrayal, arrest, and torture, he perseveres in obeying the Father. He keeps repeating the words of surrender. In the face of despair, he keeps at prayer. Fidelity to persevere in prayer at times when prayers don't seem to be answered is the way of Jesus. As followers of Jesus we need to learn to pray the same way. When we would rather be sleeping or watching television or running errands or working, Christ tries to shake us into prayer, into sitting with him for a while. Who could turn down such an invitation!

A woman of Samaria came to draw water. Jesus said to her, "Give me a drink." His disciples had gone into the town to buy food. The Samaritan woman said to him, "How can you, a Jew, ask me, a Samaritan woman, for a drink?" (For Jews use nothing in common with Samaritans.) Jesus answered and said to her, "If you knew the gift of God and who is saying to you, 'Give me a drink,' you would have asked him and he would have given you living water." [The woman] said to him, "Sir, you do not even have a bucket and the cistern is deep; where then can you get this living water? Are you greater than our father Jacob, who gave us this cistern and drank from it himself with his children and his flocks?" Jesus answered and said to her, "Everyone who drinks this water will be thirsty again; but whoever drinks the water I shall give will never thirst; the water I shall give will become in him a spring of water welling up to eternal life." The woman said to him, "Sir, give me this water, so that I may not be thirsty or have to keep coming here to draw water."

Jesus said to her, "Go call your husband and come back." The woman answered and said to him, "I do not have a husband."

Jesus answered her, "You are right in saying, 'I do not have a husband.' For you have had five husbands, and the one you have now is not your husband. What you have said is true." The woman said to him, "Sir, I can see that you are a prophet. Our ancestors worshiped on this mountain; but you people say that the place to worship is in Jerusalem." Jesus said to her, "Believe me, woman, the hour is coming when you will worship the Father neither on this mountain nor in Jerusalem. You people worship what you do not understand; we worship what we understand, because salvation is from the Jews. But the hour is coming, and is now here, when true worshipers will worship the Father in Spirit and truth; and indeed the Father seeks such people to worship him. God is Spirit, and those who worship him must worship in Spirit and truth." The woman said to him, "I know that the Messiah is coming, the one called the Anointed; when he comes, he will tell us everything." Jesus said to her, "I am he, the one who is speaking with you" (John 4:7-26).

This passage is one of the longest conversations of Jesus with anyone that is recorded in Scripture. It stands in witness to the universality of God's call and of others' response. None of the disciples expected Jesus to speak to or call a Samaritan woman, especially one with her reputation. Most women went to the well early; it was a place of social interaction. The fact that this woman was alone at a later time in the day indicates that she was an outsider even to her own. Jesus reached beyond the boundaries of society's standards to spread the Good News. This brave and honest Samaritan woman also reached beyond the same limits of society and of organized religion. She dared to listen to God in a way never heard before in her town. The key to this conversion moment was the willingness of Jesus to engage the woman in conversation and the openness of the woman to sustain the conversation against all stereotypes. Neither Jesus nor the woman should have even been talking. Yet they did; and they moved faith toward new directions and new areas.

Jesus did not see only a woman, an outsider, a public sinner. He saw a heart willing to be moved and a woman with the honesty to admit sin and the courage to change. There was a great risk for both Jesus and the woman to be seen talking publicly. Both accepted the risk and a whole town was converted. And the disciples saw another boundary stretched by the Gospel. Risk is a part of responding to Christ. At the moment of call, the risk is often paralyzing. Some cannot get beyond the apparent cost of following Christ.

This outspoken stranger at the well gives an example of how to deal with risk—just keep talking to Jesus. Regardless of what others say or think or judge, just keep up the conversation with the Son of God. Let thirst be the motivating force as it was for this woman. She needed water; she had to have it to live. Her greatness lay in the fact that she also nurtured a spirit that needed the living water. Her thirst for wholeness and peace led her into union with the giver of life. For this she risked everything, publicly and unashamedly. Following Christ carries the same risk for everyone.

Now there was a Pharisee named Nicodemus, a ruler of the Jews. He came to Jesus at night and said to him, "Rabbi, we know that you are a teacher who has come from God, for no one can do these signs that you are doing unless God is with him." Jesus answered and said to him, "Amen, amen, I say to you, no one can see the kingdom of God without being born from above." Nicodemus said to him, "How can a person once grown old be born again? Surely he cannot reenter his mother's womb and be born again, can he?" Jesus answered, "Amen, amen, I say to you, no one can enter the kingdom of God without being born of water and Spirit. What is born of flesh is flesh and what is born of spirit is spirit. Do not be amazed that I told you, 'You must be born from above.' The wind blows where it wills, and you can hear the sound it makes, but you do not know where it comes from or where it goes; so it is with everyone who is born of the Spirit" (John 3:1-8).

The story of Nicodemus is one of contrast with that of the Samaritan woman or of the women who anointed Jesus. The women did not hide their attention to Jesus. Nicodemus is fearful and goes to Jesus at night so that his Pharisee brothers won't know about it. Nicodemus had a lot to lose—his standing with the Pharisees, his reputation as a religious leader. Jesus was associated with the rabble—the poor, the uneducated, the needy, the kind of folks who will follow anyone who offers them hope. The Pharisees were above all that. Their sophistication prevented such emotional responses to a promised Messiah. They were looking for the Messiah among their own kind.

Nicodemus somehow was touched—an honest man in the midst of a pompous gathering. He went to Jesus at night. A self-righteous Messiah would have reprimanded Nicodemus for his lack of courage. Jesus took Nicodemus where he was, welcomed him, answered his questions, explained the Scriptures to him and led him into a new world of response.

Jesus does not make it too easy for Nicodemus. The following of Christ is so radical that it is a rebirth. The Spirit of God will give life in ways and places we cannot comprehend. Jesus is leading Nicodemus to respond with his intellect by his teachings and also with his whole being by his call. We use our gifts and talents to understand the ways of God, but we must go beyond mere intellect to pure faith.

Nicodemus took the steps he was able to take, and Jesus accepted the limitations of his faith and led him further. We know that Nicodemus continued to follow Christ, because we hear of his defense of Jesus before his fellow Pharisees (John 7:50-51) and his presence at Jesus' burial (John 19:39). At times when we lack the courage to follow Christ with giant steps, let the example of Nicodemus encourage us to pursue the baby steps. In time, if we persevere, the rest will follow.

But Mary stayed outside the tomb weeping. And as she wept, she bent over into the tomb and saw two angels in white sitting there, one at the head and one at the feet where the body of Jesus had been. And they said to her, "Woman, why are you weeping?" She said to them, "They have taken my Lord, and I don't know where they laid him." When she had said this, she turned around and saw Jesus there, but did not know it was Jesus. Jesus said to her, "Woman, why are you weeping? Whom are you looking for?" She thought it was the gardener and said to him, "Sir, if you carried him away, tell me where you laid him, and I will take him." Jesus said to her, "Mary!" She turned and said to him in Hebrew, "Rabbouni," which means Teacher. Jesus said to her, "Stop holding on to me, for I have not yet ascended to the Father. But go to my brothers and tell them, 'I am going to my Father and your Father, to my God and your God.'" Mary of Magdala went and announced to the disciples, "I have seen the Lord," and what he told her (John 20:11-18).

For the follower of Christ there are many calls and many responses. Life is one long response to Jesus. Mary of Magdala has already fully given herself to her Lord. She is one of the few who followed him to Calvary, risking her own life in the process. While others are in hiding after Jesus' crucifixion, Mary is at the tomb taking on the angels. She is looking for her Lord, and no one is going to stop her.

In her anxiety Mary does not recognize Jesus in front of her. In our spiritual growth Jesus leads us beyond our familiar relationship even with himself. Then Jesus calls her in a way she can never miss: "Mary." With one word she knows it is he. The intimacy, the sheer mysticism of having her Beloved speak her name. In kind, Mary responds, "Rabbouni." The only appropriate response to a personal call from the Beloved is surrender. It would appear from the Scripture that Mary was the only one at the tomb looking for her Lord. Her search and her fidelity were rewarded by the only thing she wanted—the presence of Jesus Christ.

To be pure of heart is to focus single-heartedly on Jesus Christ. He may come in ways we do not immediately recognize, but he will come and will be with us always. We have his word for that ("And behold, I am with you always, until the end of the age"—Matthew 28:20). Few of us take him at his word. Mary had always accepted her Lord, and now she was being led into a deeper acceptance—that of presence. She had searched for him all her life and had pursued him faithfully. The search is the response as fully as the finding. Mary knew that now in an unimaginable way. Her Lord was always with her. When she dashed off to tell the apostles that Jesus was risen, he was in her heart and in her steps and in her breath. Against all odds—Calvary, despair, persecution—Mary believed and loved. So did her Lord and Master, Jesus the Christ. Now they were together forever in his risen presence.

————————

> Now when they heard this [Peter's Pentecost address to the crowds], they were cut to the heart, and they asked Peter and the other apostles, "What are we to do, my brothers?" Peter [said] to them, "Repent and be baptized, every one of you, in the name of Jesus Christ for the forgiveness of your sins; and you will receive the gift of the holy Spirit. For the promise is made to you and to your children and to all those far off, whomever the Lord our God will call." He testified with many other arguments, and was exhorting them, "Save yourselves from this corrupt generation." Those who accepted his message were baptized, and about three thousand persons were added that day (Acts 2:37-41).

The uniqueness of this response is that it is communal as well as individual. Each person had to choose Jesus and be baptized, but it happened within a communal gathering. Some missionaries, especially in Africa and Asia, recognize astutely the communal aspect of faith. They preach to the whole tribe and city rather than just to individuals. They realize that people need the support of community to live the faith they profess in Christ. Christianity is such a radical departure from the standards of the world that community support is essential.

From the beginning, John the Baptist, Jesus, and now Peter proclaim the need to turn from the ways of the society in order to follow Christ. We cannot take on Christ without making significant changes in our lives. Jesus is not one of many things or people in whom we believe. Jesus is the only one, and response to him is total.

Unfortunately this passage was often used as proof that only Christians were going to heaven. The Second Vatican Council corrected that error and acknowledged that people of many faiths will be with God for all eternity.[6] But for those of us who have re-

————————

[6] Declaration of the Relation of the Church to Non-Christian Religions, *Vatican Council II: The Conciliar and Post Conciliar Documents,* Vol. 1, ed. Austin Flannery (Dublin: Dominican Publications, rev. ed. 1992), no. 1.

ceived Christ, there is no way other than his ("Jesus said to him, 'I am the way and the truth and the life. No one comes to the Father except through me'"—John 14:6). It is clear that we are redeemed by the person of Jesus Christ. Salvation comes through him. To be a follower of Christ, to be a Christian, means that we know Jesus and with him do the will of the Father. Anything that is outside the Father's will needs to be left behind. That's what Peter told the people about repentance.

The core of the response is adherence to the person of Jesus. Notice that Peter does not give a list of rules and regulations for joining the community of Christians. Peter gives the directive to repent and then believe in Jesus. It is not easy but it is simple. Put aside the things that are not of God and follow Jesus. Make the effort to get to know him and his desires. That, rather than knowledge of or compliance with rules, is the mark of a Christian.

There was a disciple in Damascus named Ananias, and the Lord said to him in a vision, "Ananias." He answered, "Here I am, Lord." The Lord said to him, "Get up and go to the street called Straight and ask at the house of Judas for a man from Tarsus named Saul. He is there praying, and [in a vision] he has seen a man named Ananias come in and lay [his] hands on him, that he may regain his sight." But Ananias replied, "Lord, I have heard from many sources about this man, what evil things he has done to your holy ones in Jerusalem. And here he has authority from the chief priests to imprison all who call upon your name." But the Lord said to him, "Go, for this man is a chosen instrument of mine to carry my name before Gentiles, kings, and Israelites, and I will show him what he will have to suffer for my name." So Ananias went and entered the house; laying his hands on him, he said, "Saul, my brother, the Lord has sent me, Jesus who appeared to you on the way by which you came, that you may regain your sight and be filled with the holy Spirit." Immediately things like scales fell from his eyes and he regained his sight. He got up and was baptized (Acts 9:10-19).

Saul had no part in God's drastic intervention in his life. Christ came to Saul in a vision, leaving him blind and helpless.

That was the call. What Saul did after that was the response. Saul did as Christ instructed—he went into Damascus and waited, praying all the time. Only Saul had the vision, so he could not prove to his friends what had happened. They could see that he was blind, but they did not see Jesus. Saul was alone in his response and he waited.

In the meantime Christ also appears to Ananias and asks him to go see Saul to heal him and baptize him. Ananias is justifiably concerned. Saul is feared, and this looks like a trick to get more Christians persecuted. But Ananias responds so that Saul also may respond. Christ uses us to speak to others. Our response determines the possibility of others also responding. Christ could have healed Saul himself just as he had blinded him. Christ chooses to involve Ananias in the work of the kingdom.

Ananias's faith is the final spark for Saul's. Ananias goes and greets Saul, "Brother Saul." Here is the man who has killed Christians with a vengeance. He is welcomed as brother by one who has suffered because of him. The scales fell from Saul's eyes at the embrace of a former enemy. From this encounter between blind Saul and faithful Ananias comes the great missionary Paul.

SECTION THREE

The Requirements

A NO TO THE THINGS THAT ARE NOT OF GOD

Your princes are rebels
    and comrades of thieves;
Each one of them loves a bribe
    and looks for gifts.
The fatherless they defend not,
    and the widow's plea does not reach them. . . .
Woe to you who join house to house,
    who connect field with field,
Till no room remains, and you are left to dwell
    alone in the midst of the land! . . .
[Woe] to those who acquit the guilty for bribes,
    and deprive the just man of his rights! (Isaiah 1:23; 5:8, 23).

Ours is an age of corporate takeovers and mergers of industrial giants. The mom-and-pop grocery store is a relic of the past, as is the local factory. Even ice cream shops are branches of large conglomerates. We call this progress. It makes for a booming economy and a rising stock market. It also leads to greater oppression of the poor and abuse of creation. Deals are made between individuals, companies, and countries that benefit the people involved and no one else. A prophet of peace can have nothing to do with this kind of legally acceptable maneuvering.

Money is an issue that every prophet has to resolve. Isaiah says that the poor and the widow come before business deals. He says the obvious: greed has no place in the kingdom. Those who accumulate wealth and drive everyone else off the land are not living God's ways. They will be alone, desolate, cut off from God and people. Bribery and cheating lead to ruin.

Money's use and illusion of power are serious matters to consider for a person called by God to be a prophet. Merely giving to good causes—churches, the poor, the sick—is not sufficient. The very making of money and the place it holds in our lives are cause for reflection and decision. The first step in the process is to examine our sources of income and see if we are honest and if others are suffering because of our pursuit of wealth.

The level of honesty required exceeds that which is lawful. It may be lawful for a company to move its production to China and employ people at slave wages to garner a huge profit margin, but it is not holy. The Christian is called to be holy. It is insufficient for a Christian to think that being honest in terms of the law is enough. The one called by God is trusted with the care of the widow, the orphan, the poor. Every step taken by a Christian needs to be measured against the standards of God not the standards of Wall Street.

For many in his day, Isaiah's words seemed absurd. Times were good; Israel was in great shape economically and politically. But they were losing it spiritually, and it was only a matter of time before the rest would crumble. Isaiah was dismissed as irrelevant and naive. Prophets today can expect the same treatment. A prayer before a business meeting doesn't cover corrupt motivation and practice. To bring God into the economic sector is to totally revamp our concept of wealth and its pursuit. Eventually the call is there to refuse to accept money as a significant power in our lives.

> Behold, the nations count as a drop in the bucket,
>> as dust on the scales;
>> the coastlands weigh no more than powder.
> Lebanon would not suffice for fuel,
>> nor its animals be enough for holocausts.
> Before him all the nations are as nought,
>> as nothing and void he accounts them (Isaiah 40:15-17).

A world tour among both the developing and the developed countries reveals that people will do anything to gain control politically. They will have coups, wars, blood baths, assassination, and intrigue of all kinds. Fortunes will be spent, and humanity will be sacrificed just so individuals can seize or win the political control of a nation, district, or region. Juxtapose this reality with Isaiah's words and there is not an iota of similarity or congruence. Children in primary school learn that apples can only be added to apples and bananas to bananas. You can't add 3 apples + 4 oranges. Political ambition and Isaiah's dictate are like apples and oranges. There is no compromise possible as they are mutually exclusive. Of course, Isaiah's words are the inspired word of God, so they are God's words. God is saying it rather simply. Political power is meaningless in the kingdom of God.

Once the shock of this wears off, certain events in society take on a new meaning. If our imaginations can envision a world in which political power is not a desired goal, what would be the result? Would human life be more precious and less expendable as a means to achieve political gains? Would some wars never have to be fought? Would the money spent on political campaigns be used for other purposes? Would people be more intent on helping one another than on stepping on each other to become the top person? The possibilities are endless. Life could be totally different.

In a world in which political power is not a goal, the needs of the people would preempt the needs of those in power. Isaiah is preaching freedom. Like other great reformers such as Jesus, Mahatma Gandhi, or Dr. Martin Luther King, Jr., Isaiah is encouraging the people to declare their freedom from those who are oppressing them. The oppression may be economic, political, or societal. Regardless of what chains others put on us, a person free before God is a free person. No one in political power can impede the work of God. They are as a drop in the bucket, and Christ is the living water that covers the whole world.

Their [the house of Jacob] land is full of silver and gold,
    and there is no end to their treasures;
Their land is full of horses,
    and there is no end to their chariots.

Their land is full of idols;
  they worship the works of their hands,
  that which their fingers have made. . . .
The haughty eyes of man will be lowered,
  the arrogance of men will be abased,
and the LORD alone will be exalted, on that day.
For the LORD of hosts will have his day
  against all that is proud and arrogant,
  all that is high, and it will be brought low;
Yes, against all the cedars of Lebanon
  and all the oaks of Bashan,
Against all the lofty mountains
  and all the high hills,
Against every lofty tower
  and every fortified wall,
Against all the ships of Tarshish
  and all stately vessels.
Human pride will be abased,
  the arrogance of men brought low,
And the LORD alone will be exalted, on that day.
The idols will perish forever (Isaiah 2:7-8, 11-18).

If the movie *The Ten Commandments* formed our idea of idols, then an idol is a golden calf to be worshiped in the desert, in which case most of us have never been tempted to idol worship. One less sin to confess! However, according to Isaiah, idols are more inclusive than that. Horses and chariots, silver and gold, the works of our hands are idols. Our own human arrogance is our idol. Anything that takes the place of God is an idol.

We could do an inventory to update Isaiah's list of possible idols. Horses and chariots are out—not a problem of them being idols. In Isaiah's day horses and chariots were a sign of military strength. Can we then make a list of our arms— nuclear and other, our personnel, all branches of the military, our defense industry, factories and think tanks? These are the chariots and horses of the third millennium. Do we put them and the silver and gold spent on them before the ways and things of God?

The works of our hands can become idols—our ambitions, goals, careers, even our families. Anything that takes priority over God is an idol. Football can be an idol. Running or swimming can be an idol. Good causes and religion can be idols. Pride can cause us to put ourselves ahead of God in many different ways in daily life. When we do, we are engaged in idol worship. Of course, we never think of it as that. We just think we overwork, overdrink, or overspend.

Isaiah shows us the God of majesty claiming rights over us as God, dismissing from the divine presence all that distracts us from God. God alone is God, and God will be exalted above all the buildings and empires and plans made by human hands. Nothing made of steel, iron, or gold can stand in the presence of the God of heaven and earth, the Creator of the stars and sun. Global companies and internet geniuses pale in the face of God. The final result of the contest between God and idols is no contest. Idols perish forever. Our souls endure forever. Why would we harness our imperishable souls to perishable objects?

But this [God's forgiveness to Nineveh] was greatly displeasing to Jonah, and he became angry. "I beseech you, LORD," he prayed, "is not this what I said while I was still in my own country? This is why I fled at first to Tarshish. I knew that you are a gracious and merciful God, slow to anger, rich in clemency, loathe to punish. And now, LORD, please take my life from me; for it is better for me to die than to live." But the Lord asked, "Have you reason to be angry?"

Jonah then left the city for a place to the east of it, where he built himself a hut and waited under it in the shade, to see what would happen to the city. And when the LORD God provided a gourd plant, that grew up over Jonah's head, giving shade that relieved him of any discomfort, Jonah was very happy over the plant. But the next morning at dawn God sent a worm which attacked the plant, so that it withered. And when the sun arose, God sent a burning east wind; and the sun beat upon Jonah's head till he became faint. Then he asked for death, saying, "I would be better off dead than alive."

But God said to Jonah, "Have you reason to be angry over the plant?" "I have reason to be angry," Jonah answered, "angry enough to die." Then the LORD said, "You are concerned over the plant which cost you no labor and which you did not raise; it came up in one night and in one night it perished. And should I not be concerned over Nineveh, the great city, in which there are more than a hundred and twenty thousand persons who cannot distinguish their right hand from their left, not to mention the many cattle?" (Jonah 4:1-11).

Condemnation is not of God. This marvelous story of Jonah allows Yahweh to reveal another side of compassion. God is compassionate to humanity without humanity deserving it. Years after the story of Jonah, Jesus Christ would give the same message with his life.

After initially running from God, Jonah has finally obeyed God's request to preach conversion to the Ninevites. Merely one day of effort on Jonah's part and the whole city from king to beggar are doing penance and praying for forgiveness from Yahweh. Resolutions to be better are flying all over Nineveh. It is a great triumph for Yahweh and for his prophet. But Jonah doesn't see it that way. He still thinks that the people of Nineveh are worthless and God shouldn't forgive them so easily.

Now Yahweh is really disgusted with Jonah. He uses the heat and the plant to remind Jonah who is in control. It seems the big fish wasn't enough. Judgment of others, which is Jonah's strong point, is not the responsibility of humanity. God alone judges, and if God chooses to be compassionate, then we have no right to condemn. Whatever the actions of others, however objectively evil they may be, God alone is judge and master of all. Our role is to proclaim the word of the Lord to believers and unbelievers, to saints and sinners, to family and foreigners. Never are we to sit under the shade of a tree and gripe because God has not struck down those we deem unworthy.

God's final, passionate plea to spare the Ninevites, his feeling of tenderness toward each of the inhabitants and even the animals, raises a standard for every person committed to God. If we are to live in peace with one another as God desires, then the self-righteous judging has to be left behind. In God all is compassion. All are given the benefit of the doubt and the opportunity to change.

> And now, why go to Egypt,
>   to drink the waters of the Nile?
> Why go to Assyria,
>   to drink the waters of the Euphrates?
> Your own wickedness chastises you,
>   your own infidelities punish you.
> Know then, and see, how evil and bitter
>   is your forsaking the LORD, your God,
> And showing no fear of me,
>   says the Lord, the GOD of hosts. . . .
> In vain I struck your children;
>   the correction they did not take.
> Your sword devoured your prophets
>   like a ravening lion (Jeremiah 2:18-19, 30).

There really is only one sin: turning our face from God. All the sins that we learned to rattle off in the confessional are specific ways of rejecting God. The Israelites in Jeremiah's time are enduring the consequences of ignoring or rejecting Yahweh. They have been busy becoming an important nation and making alliances with Assyria and Egypt. They have turned to political powers rather than to their God for strength. It isn't working. The writing on the wall spells disaster for the Israelites. These superpowers that they are courting will enslave them. God knows this, Jeremiah knows this. The people refuse to believe it.

The evil things that are happening to them are not the result of Yahweh's punishment; they are the consequences of their own actions. Life becomes miserable when we abandon God and the ways of God. We cannot blame God for the evil around us. It is not the design of God.

Jeremiah is telling us that nothing in our lives—personal, family, community, business—can be separated from God. If it is, then disaster comes; and it comes to every facet of our lives. The prophets among us do not stand on soapboxes on street corners.

They are in our daily lives. If we look we will find them at the drugstore or supermarket, the office or school, the soup kitchen or shelter. Anyone or anything that reminds us of God is a prophet. We will not find the road to peace as long as we keep ignoring them. Courage to listen to Yahweh through another human being is indeed heroic. From Jeremiah to Jesus, God chooses to speak through ordinary men and women. To close our ears to them is to close our hearts to God.

> Thus the word of the LORD came to me: Son of man, prophesy against the prophets of Israel, prophesy! Say to those who prophesy their own thought: Hear the word of the LORD: You did not step into the breach, nor did you build a wall about the house of Israel that would stand firm against attack on the day of the LORD. Was not the vision you saw false, and your divination lying? Therefore thus says the Lord GOD: Because you have spoken falsehood and have seen lying visions, therefore see! I am coming at you, says the Lord GOD.
>
> For the very reason that they led my people astray, saying, "Peace!" when there was no peace, and that, as one built a wall, they would cover it with whitewash, say then to the whitewashers: I will bring down a flooding rain; hailstones shall fall, and a stormwind shall break out. And when the wall has fallen, will you not be asked: Where is the whitewash you spread on? (Ezekiel 13:1-8).

Lying is inconsistent with peace. How many treaties that have marked the cessation of war have been founded upon lies and deceit. In time they led to more violence. A lie may be temporarily believed, but it will never last. Nothing good can come from anything built upon the lie.

Ezekiel is struggling to maintain faith while in exile in Babylon. The chosen people are being exposed to false prophets, people who were lying to them about God. These people are compared to those who put plaster on a weak wall that should be rebuilt. We all know that experience. People cover up a serious problem and pretend that it is solved, whether the problem be a relationship or a hole in the wall. A coat of paint on the ceiling doesn't repair a leaky roof.

It is not very difficult to separate the false prophets from the true prophets. Lying can never be part of God's message. No matter how painful the truth, it is the mark of God. Sometimes people lie because they say the truth would cause damage, for example, domestic violence or child abuse. The violence of those situations is already present. Lying to protect a false vision of family life only makes it worse. Eventually the wall will fall.

In a society where lying is a major part of personal, family, business, and political life, false prophets claim to be working toward peace. Actually they are working toward their own advancement and care nothing for peace. Everyone wants peace, kings and dictators included; but many want it on their terms and for their benefit. Yahweh, through Ezekiel, is reminding us that God is truth, and truth is the only way to God. There will be many false prophets offering the quick fix to difficult problems. They have no vision, no solution to life's problems. The spirit of God abides in truth. A person seeking true peace measures everything against this spirit.

When Israel was a child I loved him,
    out of Egypt I called my son.
The more I called them,
    the farther they went from me,
Sacrificing to the Baals
    and burning incense to idols.
Yet it was I who taught Ephraim to walk,
    who took them in my arms;
I drew them with human cords,
    with bands of love;
I fostered them like one
    who raises an infant to his cheeks;
Yet, though I stooped to feed my child,
    they did not know that I was their healer. . . .
How could I give you up, O Ephraim,
    or deliver you up, O Israel?
How could I treat you as Admah,
    or make you like Zeboiim?

My heart is overwhelmed,
    my pity is stirred.
I will not give vent to my blazing anger,
    I will not destroy Ephraim again;
For I am God and not man,
    the Holy One present among you;
I will not let the flames consume you (Hosea 11:1-4, 8-9).

A great stumbling block to peace is the failure of people to let God love them. This isn't a new sin, unique to our age. Hosea is trying to teach the people of his day that God loves them. The imagery is magnificent. Yahweh, the almighty God of all time and eternity, loves us as one loves a child. Yahweh draws Israel with human cords, bonds of love. And this is after Israel has resorted to idolatry, forgetting the God of their ancestors who drew them out of Egypt. They are like the people of Sodom and Gomorrah, towns that symbolize idolatry and sin. Admah and Zeboiim are the same kind of towns. Yahweh's response is a cry of love: "How could I treat you as Admah, or make you like Zeboiim?" Yahweh loves the people, even when they worship other gods and live without the one true God.

The message of Hosea is still one of the primary lessons most Christians fail to learn. God loves us. We cannot measure God's love by our own limited ability to love. We must learn to say no to thinking that we are not worthy of love. Stooping to us, God holds us close like an infant in arms. So much does God love us. God is not like us, who love only those who we feel are lovable. God is the Holy One in our midst. We have to give up our notion of being unlovable. Before we dare to extend loving hands to one another, before we are capable of loving those who reject or harm us, we must learn the peace of being held in the tender arms of God. Allowing God to love us unconditionally is a critical choice necessary for a life of union with God.

Proclaim this in the castles of Ashdod,
    in the castles of the land of Egypt:
"Gather about the mountain of Samaria,
    and see the great disorders within her,
    the oppression in her midst."

For they know not how to do what is right,
   says the LORD,
Storing up in their castles
   what they have extorted and robbed. . . .
Then will I strike the winter house
   and the summer house;
The ivory apartments shall be ruined,
   and their many rooms shall be no more,
   says the LORD. . . .
Woe to the complacent in Zion,
   to the overconfident on the mount of Samaria,
Leaders of a nation favored from the first,
   to whom the people of Israel have recourse!
   (Amos 3:9-10, 15; 6:1).

Extortion and robbery that fund domestic luxury are condemned by Amos. So much wealth is built on the backs of the poor. The industrial giants of the first half of the twentieth century made their fortunes at the expense of the lives and health of the poor who filled their factories. In unsafe buildings with poor heat, light, and ventilation, men, women, and children slaved long hours over machines that claimed many victims. This was the cost of running the steel, textile, brass, and iron mills of the country. The poor died building railroads and digging mines. If accidents didn't kill them outright, the health hazards they endured caused debilitating diseases. Union advances and federal protection laws for the safety of workers have led to the mass exodus of factories to Third World countries where the abuse can continue unabated. Cheaper goods and exorbitantly wealthy owners are the result.

That is exactly what Amos warned the people of Israel to avoid. One who is chosen by God to be prophet cannot cooperate in extortion or robbery. The warning is for all who live a high life while others suffer from abject poverty. There is no hope for peace among people as long as the disparity between rich and poor continues to grow. Amos's call is one of moderation and detachment. He is calling for divestment of wealth and integrity in acquiring it. All that Amos is condemning is socially acceptable and desirable by most. The voice of one who calls for a simple lifestyle for all is a voice that will be ignored or rebuked. It is the voice of God and deserves to be taken seriously.

———————

> I hate, I spurn your feasts,
>   I take no pleasure in your solemnities;
> Your cereal offerings I will not accept,
>   nor consider your stall-fed peace offerings.
> Away with your noisy songs!
>   I will not listen to the melodies of your harps (Amos 5:21-23).

Yahweh is angry indeed at the formalism in the religious practices of the people of Israel. Religious feasts, offerings, songs mean nothing to God without a pure heart. Trappings of religion cannot cover injustice, ingratitude, corruption, or immorality. Separate seating for blacks and whites during segregation was one glaring example of unacceptable sacrifice. How could the people of God worship God as Father and at the same time refuse to acknowledge another person as brother or sister! Sunday Mass without Monday through Saturday lives of faith quickly becomes an empty gesture.

Consider these ironies: How many wars have been fought with blessings of guns and bombs and soldiers! Can we imagine God ever blessing something that will kill another child of God? Wars themselves have been fought under the banner of the cross, the ultimate symbol of one who died nonviolently forgiving his enemies. The Second Vatican Council condemned any weapons that cause large area destruction: "Every act of war directed to the indiscriminate destruction of whole cities or vast areas with their inhabitants is a crime against God and man, which merits firm and unequivocal condemnation."[1] Nuclear weapons target large areas, yet submarines that carry nuclear weapons also carry the Eucharist.

When a baptized person accepts responsibility to be a prophet of God, daily works of justice are as important as fidelity to rules and regulations about formal worship. Can a man beat his wife or abuse his children and then come to worship every

———

[1] Pastoral Constitution on the Church in the Modern World, *Vatican Council II: The Conciliar and Post Conciliar Documents*, Vol. 1, ed. Austin Flannery (Dublin: Dominican Publications, rev. ed. 1992), no. 80.

week? What happens at the time of formal community worship is reflective of what happens the rest of the time. Liturgy is meant to be the worship that comes from the fullness of a life of faith and love. Without the faith and love, the worship is empty and anathema to God. "My sacrifice, God, is a broken spirit; / God, do not spurn a broken, humbled heart" (Psalm 51:19).

Hear this, you leaders of the house of Jacob,
    you rulers of the house of Israel!
You who abhor what is just,
    and pervert all that is right;
Who build up Zion with bloodshed,
    and Jerusalem with wickedness!
Her leaders render judgment for a bribe,
    her priests give decisions for a salary,
    her prophets divine for money,
While they rely on the LORD, saying,
    "Is not the LORD in the midst of us?
    No evil can come upon us!"
Therefore, because of you,
    Zion shall be plowed like a field,
    and Jerusalem reduced to rubble,
And the mount of the temple
    to a forest ridge (Micah 3:9-12).

Micah rails against those who abuse authority, in particular religious authority. It's hard to keep hearing over and over about the corruption of society with all the bribes and bloodshed. It fills the newspapers in every city in the world. And it would have filled the newspapers in Micah's time if they had had them.

Authority carries responsibility. In God's plan it carries a special responsibility to the poor. Unfortunately when people get power they tend to think they are all-powerful. They forget their responsibilities to God and to others. They sacrifice others' rights to achieve and maintain control. They begin to think that God works for them instead of the other way around. No one is exempt from the seduction of power. Any of us can be overbearing if given the chance.

Perhaps the key to understanding Yahweh's anger and impatience with human arrogance is in the perspective God has. God sees every creature as a beautiful, living witness to the glory of God. No one is less worthy or more worthy. Human standards tend to set the stage for some people to be more important than others, depending upon their position or accumulated wealth. That is the false premise behind some individuals lording it over others.

In this misguided self-importance, some even claim to have God on their side, in their control. Princes and priests are servants of God, not gods themselves. It is difficult to have power without being contemptuous of those who seem to have none. It is a loss of perspective as to who is God. The only way to salvation for leaders is humility in the presence of God and God's people. "LORD, my heart is not proud, / nor are my eyes haughty. / I do not busy myself with great matters, / with things too sublime for me" (Psalm 131:1).

Your hand shall be lifted above your foes,
    and all your enemies shall be destroyed.

On that day, says the LORD,
I will destroy the horses from your midst
    and ruin your chariots;
I will demolish the cities of your land
    and tear down all your fortresses (Micah 5:8-10).

Micah is one of the prophets of the remnant people, the small, unimportant group from whom the Messiah would come. His message is countercultural. It was a shock in his day and it is still one in our own time. Israel waited and prayed for a Messiah. They longed for their king to come. In the process of waiting they begged God to send them a king. God tried to convince them otherwise but gave in to their requests and sent Saul, David, and the rest. Under these kings Israel grew economically and militarily and lost spiritually. Their trust began to be placed in the power of horse and chariot and in political deals with potential enemies. They were losing the sense of trusting in God to protect and preserve them always.

Micah is called from his pasture to preach the message of trust to the people. Trust, as Micah tried to teach, is not a matter of saying prayers and offering sacrifice; trust is putting all one's energies, strength, and resources at the disposal of God. Trust, in this passage, is an act of surrender to the power of God over the power of weapons. Yahweh is angry at the people. They have spent time and treasure in the build-up of their military and have abandoned God. They seem to be about the business of seizing security. God looks upon their fortresses and strongholds in fury. They have replaced trust in God with the power of military deterrence. The futility of their efforts is clear to God but not to the people. They have become so blind to the real source of power in God that they suffer the illusion of strength from arms.

Violence can never be a source of security for any people. It gives the illusion of safety but always leads to increased violence in all areas of life. The only kingdom that has endured from the beginning of time is the kingdom of God, which is based exclusively on love. God has never used armies to proclaim, protect, or defend the reign of God on this earth. Some armies have claimed that God is behind them, as Israel did. Micah is setting the record straight. Trust in God means trust in God, not in human supports.

Woe to him who stores up what is not his:
    how long can it last!
    he loads himself down with debts. . . .
Woe to him who pursues evil gain for his household,
    setting his nest on high
    to escape the reach of misfortune! . . .
Woe to him who builds a city by bloodshed,
    and establishes a town by wickedness! . . .
Woe to you who give your neighbors
    a flood of your wrath to drink,
    and make them drunk, till their nakedness is seen! . . .
Of what avail is the carved image,
    that its maker should carve it?
Or the molten image and lying oracle,
    that its very maker should trust in it,
    and make dumb idols? (Habakkuk 2:6, 9, 12, 15, 18).

Habakkuk's warnings in this passage are similar to those of other prophets. What is unique here is that these are intended for the enemies of God's chosen people. Oppression, exploitation, violence, immorality, and idolatry are the marks of the Chaldeans, the enemies of Judah. Habakkuk is predicting that the evil the Chaldeans inflict on Judah will come back to destroy the Chaldeans themselves.

Yahweh is speaking to the people as a warning to the consequences of their own actions when they become like the Chaldeans. The names of enemies change as history moves forward, but the mark of a nation bent on self-destruction does not change. The same things that will lead to the fall of the Chaldeans will lead to the fall of Jerusalem. A people who ignore the commands of God will eventually fall apart. A people who adopt evil means become evil. A parent who cheats in business for the sake of family builds a family on lies. A community that walls out ethnic or racial diversity builds a community on hate. A nation that exploits poorer countries for economic gain builds a greedy nation. Sins initially inflicted on others will in time victimize the perpetrators.

In the work of making peace in individuals, families, communities, and countries, the people of Judah could not accept the practices of the Chaldeans. Unfortunately God's chosen people missed the main point of Habakkuk's diatribe. They saw the evil in the Chaldeans but failed to recognize the same tendencies to sin in their own actions. Claiming God on their side, they proceeded to act just as their enemies did. The double standard was alive and well. They called down the wrath of God on their enemies' evil actions, but it was okay for them to engage in violence and oppression because they had a good reason. How easily personal interests cloud the picture! It is difficult to learn not to make exceptions from God's ways for any reason.

Silence, all mankind, in the presence of the LORD! for he stirs forth from his holy dwelling (Zechariah 2:17).

There are situations in society where noise is so prevalent that it leads to extreme anxiety and even violence. Prisons can be places where the noise from televisions, prisoners, guards, metal gates and doors can be so constant that people become agitated. Inner-city building projects that house thousands of people in one block are places where it is never silent. Sirens, talking, screams, traffic, and radios blare day and night. In war just the sound of the bombs terrifies. Doctors warn that repeated exposure to loud sounds can cause permanent hearing loss.

What is obvious and measurable on the physical level also occurs on the spiritual level. Constant noise can block the word of Yahweh from penetrating to the heart. Whether the source of the noise is a radio, television or computer, the effect is the same. If days are filled with other things, there is no space for God. For many the loudest distractions come from inside. In the midst of complete external silence, our minds can race and absorb all our attention.

Zechariah's simple message is "Stop." Stop the outside and inside noise. Clear the clutter filling the ears of our body and heart. A rattled psyche can neither give nor receive peace. If we allow ourselves to be bombarded from external sounds and internal ruminations, there will be no space for the new, the different, the godlike. Every inspiration from God is a gift, undeserved and unearned. Every moment of contemplation of God is a gift, undeserved and unearned. A plant's growth is inherent in the seed. However, unless we plant and nurture the seed, the plant cannot grow. So, too, unless we provide the fertile soil for the word of God, it cannot grow within us and through us. Noise is the first rock to be cleared from the soil of our souls. The time for God ought to be exclusively for God. Everything else needs to be turned off or tuned out. The reward of doing this is inner calm. The motivation is the desire to be alert to the coming of God in our midst.

Zechariah was alerting the people to claim the vision given them by God, to prepare for the coming of the Messiah. When Jesus did come, few noticed or acknowledged him. Still in our day few see him. It is not that Jesus is not among us but that we are too busy to pay attention to him. There are many claims on our time and concern; only one is necessary.

Then Jesus was led by the Spirit into the desert to be tempted by the devil. He fasted for forty days and forty nights, and afterwards he was hungry. The tempter approached and said to him, "If you are the Son of God, command that these stones become loaves of bread." He said in reply, "It is written:
'One does not live by bread alone,
    but by every word that comes forth
        from the mouth of God.'"
Then the devil took him to the holy city, and made him stand on the parapet of the temple, and said to him, "If you are the Son of God, throw yourself down. For it is written:
'He will command his angels concerning you'
    and 'with their hands they will support you,
        lest you dash your foot against a stone.'"
Jesus answered him, "Again it is written, 'You shall not put the Lord, your God, to the test.'" Then the devil took him up to a very high mountain, and showed him all the kingdoms of the world in their magnificence, and he said to him, "All these I shall give to you, if you will prostrate yourself and worship me." At this, Jesus said to him, "Get away, Satan! It is written:
'The Lord, your God, shall you worship
    and him alone shall you serve'" (Matthew 4:1-10).

Jesus makes decisions in the desert that will determine the rest of his entire life on earth. Those decisions will eventually lead to rejection by his own people. The devil tempted Jesus with power: economic, spiritual and political. Jesus is the Messiah, but he has to decide what kind of messiah he will be.

It is clear what the people want. They want a Savior who will make them the wealthiest, most powerful nation in the world. Satan is smart and tells Jesus that material prosperity (bread from stones) is very important for a leader to be accepted. If Jesus would meet every material need of the people, he would be universally honored. Jesus says no. He knows that the human spirit is only temporarily satisfied with the fulfillment of physical needs. The psyche cries out for intimate relationship with God. Jesus came to spread the word of God, not to merely fulfill passing human needs. He is free of the power of materialism and consumerism. He is of God.

Satan returns with the carrot of control. We do like to be in control. Jesus is God and yet he does not succumb to telling God what to do. Jesus won't go for a dramatic test of power between himself and God. Jesus is here to do the will of God, not to bend the will of God to his own interests. For thousands of years individuals have sold their souls for spiritual power. It is as seductive as money. Jesus wants nothing to do with a faith that depends upon extraordinary external phenomena. He repeats his loyalty to God's will and affirms his willingness to wait for God to act. Jesus is humble and says no to forcing God's hand. Jesus is for God.

Finally Satan offers Jesus all the kingdoms of this world: full churches, universal recognition, popularity. This is a politician's dream come true. All Jesus has to do is secretly acknowledge that Satan is more powerful than God. It's a backroom deal, and no one will know about it. How many political elections have turned on such arrangements. This is the temptation to idolatry, to place someone or something before God. Jesus sees through the veneer of respectability, of good ends by sinful means. Jesus says no to the need to be universally acclaimed. He will be a Savior of the remnant by being himself a remnant person, overlooked and undervalued. Jesus will worship God and only God. He is with God always.

"[But] take care not to perform righteous deeds in order that people may see them; otherwise, you will have no recompense from your heavenly Father. When you give alms, do not blow a trumpet before you, as the hypocrites do in the synagogues and in the streets to win the praise of others. Amen, I say to you, they have received their reward. . . .

"When you pray, do not be like the hypocrites, who love to stand and pray in the synagogues and on street corners so that others may see them. Amen, I say to you, they have received their reward. . . .

"When you fast, do not look gloomy like the hypocrites. They neglect their appearance, so that they may appear to others to be fasting. Amen, I say to you, they have received their reward" (Matthew 6:1-2, 5, 16).

Holy people at the time of Jesus prayed, fasted, and gave generously to the poor. These are still the marks of a compassionate person. Every Lent the big three are prayer, fasting, and alms-giving. Fish goes on the Friday calendar, extra services are offered in the churches, and the rice bowls come out. Jesus cuts through the external action and preaches to the heart. No deed, no matter how good it looks externally, is of value if a humble heart is not behind it.

Jesus is critiquing our motivation and telling us not to flaunt supposedly religious acts. Prayer, fasting, and almsgiving are intended to be acts of worship to God. The attention is on God, not on the one offering worship. Jesus is direct and uncom-promising in his instructions in this passage. Jesus is not telling us to never do anything publicly. He is saying that public displays of good works should not be the intention of the one performing them. He is instructing us not to bother with the external if it is for our own self-aggrandizement. Our acts of religion, the exter-nal practices of our faith, are merely the overflow from a humble heart. If they are less than this, they are meaningless to God.

"Do not store up for yourselves treasures on earth, where moth and decay destroy, and thieves break in and steal. . . .

"No one can serve two masters. He will either hate one and love the other, or be devoted to one and despise the other. You cannot serve God and mammon" (Matthew 6:19, 24).

"Mammon" means money. Jesus is not cautioning us against money, because money in itself is not evil. Money is an inanimate object, neither good nor bad. Jesus knows the control money can get over people. It can destroy friendships, marriages, families, countries. Money easily becomes more important than people. It can consume our time, our efforts, our desires. That is why Jesus tells us to hate it. We were created in love and for love. Money does not create love.

When material things become the focus of our lives, we lose sight of God. There is no room in the human heart for two all-consuming treasures. Either God or possessions can fill all our being. The choice is ours. Jesus is giving us advice as to what to choose. He knows that possessions can cripple our spirits and ad-versely affect our dealings with others. We begin to value others according to their financial status. We show more respect to someone in a business suit than to someone in rags. The inordinate attachment to material things takes time away from the things of God. The wealthy spend time protecting, increasing, evaluating, and investing their resources. Often this is time taken from family, marriage, or works of mercy. Christ reminds us that wherever our treasure is, there is our heart.

"Therefore I tell you, do not worry about your life, what you will eat [or drink], or about your body, what you will wear. Is not life more than food and the body more than clothing? Look at the birds in the sky; they do not sow or reap, they gather nothing into barns, yet your heavenly Father feeds them. Are not you more important than they? Can any of you by worrying add a single moment to your life-span? Why are you anxious about clothes? Learn from the way the wild flowers grow. They do not work or spin. But I tell you that not even Solomon in all his splendor was clothed like one of them. If God so clothes the grass of the field, which grows today and is thrown into the oven tomorrow, will he not much more provide for you, O you of little faith? So do not worry and say, 'What are we to eat?' or 'What are we to drink?' or 'What are we to wear?' All these things the pagans seek. Your heavenly Father knows that you need them all. But seek first the kingdom [of God] and his righteousness, and all these things will be given you besides. Do not worry about tomorrow; tomorrow will take care of itself. Sufficient for a day is its own evil" (Matthew 6:25-34).

For anyone who has ever suffered anxiety about anything, the comment "Don't worry" triggers either despair or anger. How do you stop worrying? It seems impossible without a resolution to the problem causing the worry in the first place. In particular, anyone who has ever been poor or worked with the poor knows the reality of not having the resources to feed or clothe children or to provide medicine for the elderly. The anxiety can make you crazy. When there is no relief in sight, what do you do? It seems as if the only thing left is worry.

Jesus is trying to bring us to a higher level of trust in God. He is urging us to make concrete acts of trust about real needs in daily life. Jesus brings us into the present moment and tries to extricate us from the trap of anxiety about tomorrow's worries. Whatever is happening to us at the present is not happening to us alone. Christ is with us. Pain, suffering, death, disaster, loss, fear, or whatever else is causing us the mind-numbing worry is not stronger than the life of Christ and his presence with us. Specifically how can we learn to live this way? The only way to trust God when panic overtakes us is to begin to practice trust. At the moment the worry crashes in on us, make an act of trust in God. Every time the worry hits, so also will the act of trust. God will lead us from fear to trust. Christ will develop in us a spirit of trust that will permeate others and heal our own souls.

"Stop judging, that you may not be judged. For as you judge, so will you be judged, and the measure with which you measure will be measured out to you. Why do you notice the splinter in your brother's eye, but do not perceive the wooden beam in your own eye? How can you say to your brother, 'Let me remove that splinter from your eye,' while the wooden beam is in your eye? You hypocrite, remove the wooden beam from your eye first; then you will see clearly to remove the splinter from your brother's eye" (Matthew 7:1-5).

Whenever we judge another person, we assume the responsibility that belongs to God alone. Only God knows the human heart, so only God can judge. Christ teaches us wisdom, the wisdom of knowing ourselves. He reminds us that our own desires and ambitions can prevent us from seeing other situations and other people objectively. Even when personal emotions are not involved, cultural conditioning and life experiences limit us. In some Arab countries it is an insult to shake hands with the right hand; in some Western countries it is an insult not to. If two individuals from each of those areas did not know that, it is possible that they would insult each other while trying to be polite.

If simple customs can be problematic, what of the effects of sin and human weakness? We see a car ram our wall and we curse the driver. We may not have seen the driver avoid hitting a child.

Our jumping to blame was misguided by our concern about the wall. Let us take a more extreme matter. A person commits a heinous crime—the murder of a child. There is no justification for such action. Still, the judgment is not ours to make. Christ says, "Do not judge." Leaving the judgment to God, however, does not mean that we ignore evil. We must personally and communally resist evil in all its forms. At the same time that we work actively against objective evil and try to prevent its continuation, we do not judge the person committing the evil. The action can be judged but not the person.

Anger that leads to judgment and judgment that leads to condemnation create the beginning of divisions that separate one from another. In time these divisions can lead to gossip, ostracizing, violence, and war. Lives are torn apart by the judgments of others. Whole families or nations are excluded from our friendship because of the judgment we pass on some individuals. Injustice and oppression of any kind can be condemned, but the perpetrators of such evil are always our brothers and sisters. We always love them at the same time that we resist their actions.

Christ's words are not complex. God alone is the judge of the living and the dead. We are not capable of assuming that task.

Jesus sent out these twelve [apostles] after instructing them thus . . . "Do not take gold or silver or copper for your belts; no sack for the journey, or a second tunic, or sandals, or walking stick. The laborer deserves his keep" (Matthew 10:5, 9, 10).

The ability to say no to certain things can free a person for other things. Jesus is sending out his apostles to proclaim the kingdom. He wants them to go freely and to rejoice in the kingdom without concern for mundane realities of daily life. Jesus tells them not to take money, thus freeing them from thinking that financial backing is necessary for the spread of the word of God. Think of all the great works of charity that have been founded upon faith alone.

Jesus tells them not to take extra clothes, thus freeing them from worrying about protecting themselves. Without a knapsack they are more free to get up and go at once when the spirit moves them. Watch people travel in an airport or bus stop. Some have so much baggage that they are weighed down by it. Dragging it around can make a vacation burdensome. The apostles were to bring the Gospel, not anything else. The trappings of a culture can inhibit the Gospel, as many missionaries have learned.

An extra pair of sandals is not necessary. If something happens along the way, the apostles will have to be dependent upon the people to whom they are preaching. The apostles will be vulnerable to both God and to the people. By their freedom from visible means of support, they are proclaiming the invisible God. If God cannot be trusted with the needs of our daily life, how can God be trusted with our hearts and souls! In the 1960s the expression "The medium is the message" was popular. Jesus is teaching us that the way we live and move is as much the preaching of the Gospel as what we say. The word of God stands on its own without the need for external support.

Then Jesus said to his disciples, "Whoever wishes to come after me must deny himself, take up his cross, and follow me. For whoever wishes to save his life will lose it, but whoever loses his life for my sake will find it. What profit would there be for one to gain the whole world and forfeit his life? Or what can one give in exchange for his life?" (Matthew 16:24-26).

Jesus has asked his followers to give up money, power, judgment, self-righteousness, anxiety, and all visible means of support. This passage contains all that and more. Jesus asks us to die to ourselves and to rise again with him. For each person the call to die to self will be as unique as fingerprints. It is a call inherent in our baptism. The sacrament, by its nature, implies rebirth.

The denying of self does not degrade humanity as created by God. It brings it to its greatest fulfillment. We are most fully ourselves when we live in God. Denying ourselves for Christ's sake increases our stature as human beings. Denial of self means that everything we do or pursue is measured against the criteria of God's will. If God gives me a good meal, I rejoice. If God lets me fast, I rejoice. Eating and fasting are neither good nor bad in themselves. The grace to be free of bondage to food or to fasting is holiness. If God gives me good health, I rejoice. If God allows sickness, I rejoice.

The continual conversion of self to God is the denial Jesus is addressing. Over and over in our lives, we surrender our own desires and will to God's. Sometimes these conversions are dramatic; often they are minor. The process of surrendering in all things is the important part. The transformation of the individual into Christ, accomplished only by a death to self, is the foundation of the transformation of the world into the kingdom of God.

Great crowds were traveling with him, and he turned and addressed them, "If any one comes to me without hating his father and mother, wife and children, brothers and sisters, and even his own life, he cannot be my disciple. Whoever does not carry his own cross and come after me cannot be my disciple" (Luke 14:25-27).

Abused children carry a love/hate relationship with their parents throughout their lives. Jesus is not talking about that kind of familial hatred. He is speaking of detachment, of initiative, of independence, of freedom. Everything that Jesus teaches is intended for the good of the kingdom and the good of the individual. Christ's challenge is not suggesting a rift in families for his sake. It is a call to be unique, to be free of others' expectations, to grow into the persons we are called to be by our creation by God and re-creation in Christ's baptism.

Children can live their entire lives under the domination of their parents' culture and social standing. Children who pursue careers chosen for them by their parents will never be happy in their jobs. Christ knows this and encourages each person to take the time to discover who he or she is before God and then to surrender to that call even in the face of resistance from family members.

In the extreme, many individuals who have embraced Catholicism have been cut off from their family ties and inheritance. Men and women through the ages have entered religious life over severe objections and censures from family members. Young couples have married outside their parents' limited, socially acceptable class and been ostracized for it. Martyrs have given their lives for the faith. People have lost jobs, careers, and reputations for the sake of truth. The bottom line is that we are called by Jesus Christ to be free of anything that prohibits a free and total following of him. Obviously we are not called to hate those who oppose us, but we are meant to act according to the truth of our own conscience regardless of who opposes us. Our primary accountability is to God.

"Whoever causes one of these little ones who believe in me to sin, it would be better for him to have a great millstone hung around his neck and to be drowned in the depths of the sea. Woe to the world because of things that cause sin! Such things must come, but woe to the one through whom they come! If your hand or foot causes you to sin, cut it off and throw it away. It is better for you to enter into life maimed or crippled than with two hands or two feet to be thrown into eternal fire. And if your eye causes you to sin, tear it out and throw it away. It is better for you to enter into life with one eye than with two eyes to be thrown into fiery Gehenna.

"See that you do not despise one of these little ones, for I say to you that their angels in heaven always look upon the face of my heavenly Father" (Matthew 18:6-10).

Jesus' usual compassionate manner of speaking takes a drastic turn in this section. When it comes to children, he is fiercely protective, as a loving parent. He chastises adults and warns of the dire consequences to giving a bad example to children. As people committed to peace, the issue of our example of peacefulness to our children is indeed serious and in need of improvement on most fronts.

To expose our children to violence and hatred in the media, in sports, in family quarrels, in business dealings, in speech, and in every other area of life is to scandalize them. Surrounding them with violence causes children to become fearful and combative. In the ancient Iroquois tribal practice, there were always elderly people whose responsibility it was to measure every decision the tribe made against its effect on the children. It was an immediate protection against short-term gain and long-term loss.

So serious is our commitment to our children that we would be better off maimed than continuing to scandalize them. Christ is calling his followers to a higher standard than good parenting, although that is a by-product. He is reminding us that we do not sin alone. Every sin brought into the world through our actions has a ripple effect that permeates our environment. Children are the most susceptible to the adverse effects of sin. It can stunt their spiritual and moral growth to a high degree. Squarely and firmly Christ places the blame for this on the adults. In a world where one third of our children are abused, where more than half are hungry, where millions are refugees from war, we have a great deal to answer for.

A YES TO THE THINGS THAT ARE OF GOD

> "For this command which I enjoin on you today is not too mysterious and remote for you. It is not up in the sky, that you should say, 'Who will go up in the sky to get it for us and tell us of it, that we may carry it out?' Nor is it across the sea, that you should say, 'Who will cross the sea to get it for us and tell us of it, that we may carry it out?' No, it is something very near to you, already in your mouths and in your hearts; you have only to carry it out. . . .
>
> "I call heaven and earth today to witness against you: I have set before you life and death, the blessing and the curse. Choose life, then, that you and your descendants may live, by loving the LORD, your God, heeding his voice, and holding fast to him. For that will mean life for you, a long life for you to live on the land which the LORD swore he would give to your fathers Abraham, Isaac and Jacob" (Deuteronomy 30:11-14, 19-20).

The primary yes of every person who believes in the God of Abraham and of the same God of our Lord Jesus Christ is the yes to life itself, to the primacy of God as author of life and to God as sustainer of life. This is the essential question every believer must ask in the presence of God. The answer to this question is the basis for every action of daily life and for every decision involving life itself.

Before we consider abortion, before God we ask if this choice is a choice for life. Before we condemn a convicted person to death, before God we ask if this choice is a choice for life. Before we bear arms for a political state against a country's enemies, before God we ask if this is a choice for life. Before we engage in the business of oppressing workers for profit, before God we ask if this is a choice for life. Before we confine our elderly to poor health care and days of loneliness, before God we ask if this is a choice for life. Before we dismiss the homeless as someone else's problem, before God we ask if this is a choice for life.

God is decisive in standing for life. As children of God we must be as decisive in every aspect of human life. The choice for life is more than a single-issue agenda. It embraces the call to be willing to struggle through the gray parts of daily life and human existence. The black-and-white issues such as murder and adultery are easy to recognize as outside the commands of God. Our journey through life is a process of discovering that the choice to life reaches into the very depths of our psyches and the minute details of our days. It is in the small decisions of the day that we progress in the great choice for life.

> Wash yourselves clean!
> Put away your misdeeds from before my eyes;
> cease doing evil; learn to do good.
> Make justice your aim: redress the wronged,
> hear the orphan's plea, defend the widow (Isaiah 1:16-17).

Yahweh spells out the path of the holy person. Step 1: Stop doing ugly and hurtful things. Step 2: Practice doing beautiful and helpful things. Specifically, take on justice as a personal responsibility. Make a mark on changing the ills of society. Help the unfortunate who have no one else. The orphans are those children who are without parents and also all those who have been orphaned by the circumstances of life, who have no guidance, no support, no recourse. Defend the widowed. In Isaiah's time a widow had no means of support and was totally dependent upon the kindness of others to sustain life. There are many in society today who are nakedly vulnerable with no one to stand up for them. The infirm, the elderly, the mentally ill, the poor, the addicted, the young, the imprisoned—these are the widows of today.

Isaiah is presenting a plan of action for a lifetime. If being a disciple of God meant only not doing bad things, Isaiah wouldn't have had to preach. The chosen people already had the commandments. Isaiah's responsibility was to bring the spirit of the commandments into everyday political and social life. The overriding sense here is one of action. God wants us to do something about the problems people have to face. We are expected to speak out, to initiate, to motivate, to assist.

These directives from God through Isaiah are intended for all the people of God. For many this is an adjustment, a switch from leaving the radical works of mercy to the missionaries and religious and bringing it home to every single baptized Christian. Parishes and schools have committees for peace and justice. Isaiah preaches that the entire Church is commissioned to be a proclaimer of peace and prophet of justice.

> He shall judge between the nations,
>   and impose terms on many peoples.
> They shall beat their swords into plowshares
>   and their spears into pruning hooks;
> One nation shall not raise the sword against another,
>   nor shall they train for war again (Isaiah 2:4).

Folk singers have adopted this cry from Isaiah more than church people. The word of God is intended for all people. How few ever accept the responsibility to do what God is asking in this passage. Desiring peace is not enough; neither is praying for it. Isaiah says we must do peace, take the things of hatred, violence, and war and destroy them. Make peace a priority. Transform industries of destruction into industries of construction.

Perhaps the first issue raised by Isaiah is a metamorphosis of perception. To embrace the word of God means first of all to imagine it as a possibility and then accept it as a responsibility. At times of war people quickly jump to the patriotic side, professing support

of those risking their lives in the fighting. To criticize the war is to
incur the wrath of those who support it. Always justice is on our
side, regardless of which side we are on. Discussions abound as to
the justification of any particular confrontation that warrants a
military response. We are asked to submit our consciences to those
who know better—the political leaders and the generals.

In faith we are to submit our conscience to God and to God
alone. If God asks us to give up the things of war and to find
ways to bring peace to any situation, then we are obliged to do
that. No state, no government, no national security need over-
rides the word of God. We may not know how to make peace in
any given situation, but we certainly know, by these words of
Yahweh through Isaiah, that we are called to work at it.

> I, the LORD, have called you for the victory of justice,
>   I have grasped you by the hand;
> I formed you, and set you
>   as a covenant of the people,
>   a light for the nations,
> To open the eyes of the blind,
>   to bring out prisoners from confinement,
>   and from the dungeon, those who live in darkness.
> I am the LORD, this is my name;
>   my glory I give to no other,
>   nor my praise to idols (Isaiah 42:6-8).

If and when a blood brother or sister or cousin or relative of
any kind is imprisoned, whether justly or unjustly, awareness
of the whole prison scene breaks open before us. The darkness of
confinement is experienced. Or if we ourselves are in jail, the
darkness threatens us on all sides. The vulnerability, the helpless-
ness, the total lack of privacy, and, in some cases, the abuse from
the guards or other prisoners, the embarrassment, and the sense
of failure can overwhelm anyone behind bars for any reason. Prisons are places of punishment; there is little about them that
speaks of compassion and covenant. They degrade the human
spirit and often violate the human body.

Isaiah preaches another covenant that no human confinement can prohibit. No shackle can prevent us from grasping the Lord's hand. Solitary confinement cannot keep the Lord away. The light of Christ reaches into the most darkened hellhole in the world's worst prison. When the first nuclear explosion occurred at White Sands Missile Site on July 16, 1945, a blind girl said she saw a brilliant light for the first and only time in her life. Yahweh is infinitely more powerful than a nuclear explosion. And it is the light of God that we are sent to bring to anyone in darkness and to experience ourselves when we are in darkness.

A start could be to actually reach out to those in prison for whatever reason. Some will be able to visit, others can correspond. There are people in jail who have no outside contacts. Their whole lives become the four walls of their cell. The only people they ever communicate with are other prisoners or the guards. Despair and anger are constant temptations. Unless someone teaches them by personal compassion that there is a God who desires to take them by the hand and form them, they will never know the light of Christ. The word of God breaks through prison walls as easily as it did for Peter (Acts 12:5-11).

Isaiah foretold the coming of the Messiah, and one of the signs of his presence would be freedom for prisoners. Society may confine alleged perpetrators of violence and other illegal acts, but no one who bears the light of Christ can judge, condemn, or ignore their brother or sister in jail.

If you hold back your foot on the sabbath
    from following your own pursuits on my holy day;
If you call the sabbath a delight,
    and the LORD's holy day honorable;
If you honor it by not following your ways,
    seeking your own interests, or speaking with malice—
Then you shall delight in the LORD,
    and I will make you ride on the heights of the earth;
I will nourish you with the heritage of Jacob, your father,
    for the mouth of the LORD has spoken (Isaiah 58:13-14).

Time is one of life's greatest commodities. One of technology's constant pursuits is devices to save time. Today there exist millions of inventions that do just that. Yet our age is one of constant stress for most people, who cannot do all they expect within their everyday life. Sunday or Sabbath Day is just another day. Even for those who still worship regularly, there is little difference between the rush of Sunday and the rush of the weekdays. The work being done may not be at the office, but it is still work. For some work is at the touch of a cell phone or computer. Stores are open on Sunday just as they are any other day.

The choice to make holy the Sabbath is personal. Society has no boundaries, so individuals must be the ones to make the choices as to how to spend time. Leisure is one of God's great gifts to us through the Jewish people. Until the chosen people received the revelation to take one day of rest and prayer, the idea of such a day was unheard of in ancient times. Yahweh is reminding people that God needs to be acknowledged to such a degree that one day a week ought to be exclusively dedicated to God. Yahweh is also reminding people that they are worthy of a day without the burden of work, that their spirits need the time to recover and recreate themselves. Attending to God is the way to become more fully human.

A simple reflection on behavioral attitudes of drivers on highways or shoppers in a supermarket shows the effect of stress in life. Spousal relationships, child-raising, friendships, and health all suffer the effects of people trying to do too much. If a husband or wife does not have the time or energy to have a civil conversation or to be patient with a child, how can that person relate to God?

There is a critical proportionality between the choices we make in allocating our time during the week and the way we spend the Sabbath. A renewal of the Sabbath begins with a renewal of time in general. Priorities are measurable. If we spend all our waking hours at work, then work is the most important reality in our lives. If we never take a moment to think of God or talk to God during the week, then we won't know what to do with God on Sunday. Many complain that Mass or other Sunday worship is not meaningful or relevant. The nature of the service may be an issue, but the major reason is not the worship service but the week preceding it.

What kind of a marriage would a couple have if they met for one hour a week? What kind of parenting would a child have if the parents were available only one hour a week? How can we know God if one hour a week is all the time we give to the relationship? We are called to be free people born to celebrate the reign of God in our midst, not to be slaves to our work and consumer society. Sabbath-keeping is the way to let God teach us to "ride the heights of the earth."

> The spirit of the Lord GOD is upon me,
>   because the LORD has anointed me;
> He has sent me to bring glad tidings to the lowly,
>   to heal the brokenhearted,
> To proclaim liberty to the captives
>   and release to the prisoners,
> To announce a year of favor from the LORD
>   and a day of vindication by our God,
>   to comfort all who mourn;
> To place on those who mourn in Zion
>   a diadem instead of ashes,
> To give them oil of gladness in place of mourning,
>   a glorious mantle instead of a listless spirit.
> They will be called oaks of justice,
>   planted by the LORD to show his glory (Isaiah 61:1-3).

What an incredible mission Isaiah has been given! Of course, the same mission became the defining description of the Messiah. Jesus claimed these words of Isaiah to identify himself (Luke 4:14-22). Because these words were fulfilled in Jesus, they are thereby fulfilled in us. We are one with Christ by our baptism, so his mission is our mission.

The majority of the world's population have never heard of Christ. They have no idea of the joy and peace of Christ in their lives. The challenge is laid for those who do know Christ and have been given the gift of faith to spread this word to all people in all places at all times. The brokenhearted, the despairing, the walking wounded of society are the fertile ground awaiting the seed of Christ's word.

Missionaries from the time of Paul and Peter have given themselves selflessly for the sake of the spread of the kingdom. Somewhere down the centuries a misconception developed that missionaries were nuns, priests, brothers, or laypersons who went to foreign countries to serve God's poor and bring them the Gospel. The rest of us supported them by our prayers and money.

If we use the same criterion—travel to a foreign country—Jesus wouldn't classify as a missionary. He never traveled more than fifty miles from the place of his birth. Most of his preaching was to his own people. He assumed the mission foretold by Isaiah in his hometown in the region of Galilee. The same sense of mission is inherent in our baptismal consecration, our time of anointing. Few of us think of ourselves as freeing the oppressed, healing the ill, consoling the sorrowful, setting prisoners free. There is no place in Christianity for a false sense of humility. We are called to do great and awesome things through the power of God working in us. We are Christ and his mission is our mission.

Jonah began his journey through the city, and had gone but a single day's walk announcing, "Forty days more and Nineveh shall be destroyed," when the people of Nineveh believed God; they proclaimed a fast and all of them, great and small, put on sackcloth.

When the news reached the king of Nineveh, he rose from his throne, laid aside his robe, covered himself with sackcloth, and sat in the ashes. Then he had this proclaimed throughout Nineveh, by decree of the king and his nobles: "Neither man nor beast, neither cattle nor sheep, shall taste anything; they shall not eat, nor shall they drink water. Man and beast shall be covered with sackcloth and call loudly to God; every man shall turn from his evil way and from the violence he has in hand. Who knows, God may relent and forgive, and withhold his blazing wrath, so that we shall not perish." When God saw by their actions how they turned from their evil way, he repented of the evil that he had threatened to do to them; he did not carry it out.

But this was greatly displeasing to Jonah, and he became angry (Jonah 3:4–4:1).

There are two responses to God's call in this passage. The first is the response of repentance, expressed in a physical way—prayer and fasting. The second is that of accepting the compassion of God for others. Poor old Jonah had trouble with both.

After a stopover in the fish's belly because of his refusal to preach to the Ninevites, Jonah finally acquiesces to God's will. Jonah begins what he expects to be a three days' journey across Nineveh to chastise the inhabitants and warn them of God's anger with them. Only one day into the journey the whole country, from king to lowliest beast, takes up mass repentance and serious fasting. They know they have messed up their lives and offended God, and they are sorry. They express it physically by wearing sackcloth and ashes, the official garb of the repentant sinner. Yahweh is moved with pity for them and forgives them completely.

Now Jonah is really displeased. These low-life people of Nineveh are too bad for God to ever forgive. Such is the judgment of Jonah. This moves us into the second lesson of the story: God is allowed to be merciful to anyone. The degree and number of sins are irrelevant to the mercy of God. And Jonah has to learn this. When we sin we need to express our sincere repentance with our bodies. The way we express it can be as unique as each of us is. It can be prayer, fasting, sacrifice, almsgiving, visiting the sick, or any other action that speaks of a turning of our heart to God. And then we must believe that God forgives completely. Our sins are taken away forever by the mercy of God. No sin is too great, no person too evil, for the embrace of our compassionate God.

A critical aspect of being a peacemaker like Christ is to allow others the opportunity to change and then to celebrate their freedom from sin or violence. Jesus himself told us the appropriate response to a repentant sinner: "In just the same way, I tell you, there will be rejoicing among the angels of God over one sinner who repents" (Luke 15:10). Rejoicing in God's mercy is a choice for the Christian.

For to the men of Judah and to Jerusalem, thus says the LORD:
Till your untilled ground,
  sow not among thorns.

> For the sake of the LORD, be circumcised,
>> remove the foreskins of your hearts,
>> O men of Judah and citizens of Jerusalem;
> Lest my anger break out like fire,
>> and burn till none can quench it,
>> because of your evil deeds (Jeremiah 4:3-4).

Jeremiah was an industrious prophet at a time of great difficulty for the chosen people. They didn't want to hear Jeremiah's message because he was telling them that they had turned from the things of God and disaster was about to befall them, as it does any of us who turn from God. Hopefully we have moved from the false notion of a revenging God keeping track of our offenses and punishing us accordingly. The disaster that happens when we sin is not the work of God but the consequences of sin itself.

If by free will we sin, then by free will we can turn from sin. This is the point of Jeremiah's plea to his people. If they want to reap the fruits of a life with God, then they must work at it. A farmer who does no work is either rich enough to have someone do the work for him or else he has an unproductive farm. The ground must be chosen carefully for its ability to produce a crop, and then it must be tilled and fertilized. So it is with God's word in our hearts. It takes effort to prepare the fertile soil for the seed of God to grow. We are the ones who put out the effort.

As the Jewish people were obliged to circumcise their male children, so also were they to remove the outer layer of their hearts as part of their dedication to God. Circumcision was for them the physical symbol of surrender to God. Jeremiah is the first of many prophets who will warn people that no physical act, no matter how holy, is meaningful unless the heart is also focused on God. The sign of a chosen race was not the circumcised males but the circumcised hearts. "For in Christ Jesus, neither circumcision nor uncircumcision counts for anything, but only faith working through love" (Galatians 5:6). Surrender as total and as irreversible as physical circumcision is the tilling of the ground for the seed of God to grow.

It is not enough to sit back and wait for the reign of God to pop up and surprise us. We are responsible for helping to bring it about. As the farmer works in his field day by day, so we work continuously toward the time when the peace and love of God will be in every heart and every home. God's gracious generosity and our constant cooperation together create a world of love.

———————

> For I know well the plans I have in mind for you, says the LORD, plans for your welfare, not for woe! plans to give you a future full of hope. When you call me, when you go to pray to me, I will listen to you. When you look for me, you will find me. Yes, when you seek me with all your heart, you will find me with you, says the LORD, and I will change your lot; I will gather you together from all the nations and all the places to which I have banished you, says the LORD, and bring you back to the place from which I have exiled you (Jeremiah 29:11-14).

The Jerusalem Bible translates the first verse of this passage as: "I know the plans I have in mind for you—it is Yahweh who speaks—plans for peace, not disaster, reserving a future full of hope for you." An incredible statement given to a people about to experience the fall of their beloved Jerusalem! A people about to be conquered and taken into slavery are being reminded that this is not the plan of God. War, destruction, murder, rape, and suffering are not God's creations or God's plans. Always God desires peace and security for the people. When there is not peace, then it is the work of men and women, not the plan of God.

Jeremiah is telling the people to never stop trusting in Yahweh, to never stop believing in a future full of hope. The chosen people will have to remember these words through long years of despairing slavery. In the midst of trying circumstances, when all seems hopeless, Yahweh will be present, listening to the pleas of the people. The cries of mortal anguish will reach the heart of God. The response Jeremiah is teaching the people in these words is to pray always, to trust in God always, to count on God's presence always. But the prayers are more than words said. The prayers are the cries from a soul seeking God with every fiber of being. The seeker will find God present and will journey toward the day when the plans of God are fulfilled.

At that time, says the LORD
 I will be the God of all the tribes of Israel,
 and they shall be my people.
 Thus says the LORD:
The people that escaped the sword
 have found favor in the desert.
As Israel comes forward to be given his rest,
 the LORD appears to him from afar:
With age-old love I have loved you;
 so I have kept my mercy toward you.
Again I will restore you, and you shall be rebuilt,
 O virgin Israel;
Carrying your festive tambourines,
 you shall go forth dancing with the merry-makers.
Again you shall plant vineyards
 on the mountains of Samaria;
 those who plant them shall enjoy the fruits.
Yes, a day will come when the watchmen
 will call out on Mount Ephraim:
"Rise up, let us go to Zion,
 to the LORD, our God" (Jeremiah 31:1-6).

During Jeremiah's time of prophecy, the tribes of Israel were divided among themselves. Times were hard, and there are many chapters of lamentation in the book of Jeremiah. This passage is not one of them; it is at the beginning of the chapters of consolation. Unity is the theme for the time of peace and prosperity promised by Yahweh—unity with God and with one another. We cannot be divided one from another and be at peace with God; and we cannot be divided from God and be at peace with one another. Only when the tribes of Israel are reunited can any of them experience peace.

Yahweh will console the chosen people, but the consolation will be for all the people, not for one tribe over another. How often do we pray for peace at the expense of another nation. It happens all the time during war. One country prays for the end of the fighting on their terms—victory for their side. An opposing country prays in the same way. What kind of a God would we have who would answer one country's prayers at the expense of the other? The Israelites were like us. They wanted God on their own terms. God will answer their prayers, but it will be in the reality of unity among all people. Division among people cannot coexist with the peace of Christ. Efforts to understand and accept differences in culture and race and temperament accompany the person striving for peace.

Yahweh is promising the people and us that we can learn to accept all people. When that day comes, we will be rebuilt as the people of God, the people whom God has always loved. Though our sins have been many and infidelities to the true God numerous, we will all be virgins of Israel, adorned by our God in robes of peace and light. Celebration will follow as the sign of a free person aware of the everlasting love of God. After the end of hostilities people gather in the streets to celebrate the presence of peace. Often the peace is short-lived and temporary. When the peace of God comes, there will be no end to the celebration. Tambourines and dancing in the streets will proclaim the reign of God in our midst.

> Away with your noisy songs!
> I will not listen to the melodies of your harps.
> But if you would offer me holocausts,
> then let justice surge like water,
> and goodness like an unfailing stream.
> Did you bring me sacrifices and offerings
> for forty years in the desert, O house of Israel? (Amos 5:23-25).

It sounds as though Yahweh doesn't like music. That is hardly the case. Songs and instruments were the style of prayer for the Hebrew people. When they were in the desert, their worship was more simple and their hearts more focused. It's rather hard to be elaborate when you are nomadic. Seasoned travelers always carry as little baggage as possible. The years of wandering in the desert were a time of prayer and sensitivity to the word of God. The desert experience in Scripture is usually associated with union with God.

Simplicity of worship is part of this experience. Ritual and style conform to the barren landscape. Only the essential is necessary.

Amos is reminding the people who have now settled on a land of their own that what they have added in liturgical practices they have lost in sincerity. They act as if the quality of the worship ritual is more important than the quality of their lives of charity. Justice and integrity, not chants and harps, are the essentials of worship. Over and over in the history of salvation God has to remind people that the external is only important as a reflection of the internal. Hearts open to the needs and rights of others are hearts that know how to worship. Liturgical training in any age has never been the source of true worship. That has always been the fruit of a life of honesty toward others. The measure of our prayer is the measure of our integrity with our brothers and sisters.

> As for you, son of man, speak to the house of Israel: You people say, "Our crimes and our sins weigh us down; we are rotting away because of them. How can we survive?" Answer them: As I live, says the Lord GOD, I swear I take no pleasure in the death of the wicked man, but rather in the wicked man's conversion, that he may live. Turn, turn from your evil ways! Why should you die, O house of Israel? (Ezekiel 33:10-11).

There is courage in knowing ourselves. St. Teresa of Avila and St. John of the Cross both stressed that the basis of spiritual growth is self-knowledge. Ezekiel is dealing with a people who have seriously snubbed Yahweh. They have been living immoral lives, worshiping idols, practicing dishonesty in all their business dealings, and basically ignoring all the commands of God. Some think there is no hope for them because of the extent of their sins. Ezekiel is reminding them that Yahweh is a God of life not death. There is never a reason to despair of God's assistance and love.

Seeing sin as sin is a great grace. Ezekiel is preparing the people for this grace. Too often we justify sin as necessary or label it as "not that bad." The excuses are legion: "I'm too busy to go to church." "My marriage was over long before I started the affair." "It's their own fault they are poor; I don't have to help them." "Everyone cheats on taxes." "We didn't start the war." The moment of truth when sin is seen for what it is—a refusal to love and be loved—is the crisis moment when the opportunity to choose is present.

Sin is not a popular word these days. But to acknowledge our actions as outside the desire of God is the beginning of salvation. Yahweh clearly speaks of life and hope for the sinner. Following recognition of sinfulness comes the choice to repent, to turn to other ways of living. Change is painfully difficult. It doesn't just happen by itself. A decision to change, to repent, is the start. Once that is made, the journey of conversion begins. The pace is usually slow. Like a beginning marathon runner in training, the primary concern is consistency, not speed. We begin step by step, mile by mile, relearning life according to God's standards. The journey is the journey of life, and God is present for all of it.

Then these three in the furnace with one voice sang, glorifying and blessing God:

"Blessed are you, O Lord, the God of our fathers,
    praiseworthy and exalted above all forever;
And blessed is your holy and glorious name,
    praiseworthy and exalted above all for all ages.
Blessed are you in the temple of your holy glory,
    praiseworthy and glorious above all forever.
Blessed are you on the throne of your kingdom,
    praiseworthy and exalted above all forever. . . .
Hananiah, Azariah, Mishael, bless the Lord;
    praise and exalt him above all forever.
For he has delivered us from the nether world,
    and saved us from the power of death;
He has freed us from the raging flame
    and delivered us from the fire.
Give thanks to the Lord, for he is good,
    for his mercy endures forever. . . .
Bless the God of gods, all you who fear the Lord;
    praise him and give him thanks,
    because his mercy endures forever" (Daniel 3:51-54, 88-90).

Gratitude and praise of God well up from the hearts and mouths of Hananiah, Azariah, and Mishael as they dance amidst the flames of the overheated furnace. Finding themselves in an apparent no-win situation with King Nebuchadnezzar, they had been expecting to die. The king had ordered all the inhabitants of Babylon to prostrate themselves and worship a golden statue representing one of the pagan gods. These three young Hebrew men refused even when threatened with a trip through the fiery furnace. They boldly told the king that their God could save them. Even if God did not save them, they would rather die than worship false gods.

Their courage preceded their rescue. The sequence of events is important. Faith precedes salvation. Now in the fire without being burned, the young men were delighted with God and with themselves. They were alive and more than alive. They were alive only because their God loved them. They danced and sang, praising, glorifying, and thanking God.

This passage is only part of the entire hymn of praise from the furnace; it is the beginning and the end. The verses in between praise God through every detail and creature of heaven and earth. Once they recognize God as the source of all life, especially theirs, Hananiah, Azariah, and Mishael see the entire world and its inhabitants as reflections of the goodness and love of the Creator. They can't keep from singing. Praise and gratitude to God are part and parcel of a life committed to bringing about the realm of God on this earth. If we look at the earth and society around us as belonging to us, then we fail to see them in their true light. Although many events and realities are the consequences of human choices and actions, the universe is made by God and destined to be fulfilled in God.

If we hold the fragile universe in the reverence that Hananiah, Azariah, and Mishael held it, we would be less likely to destroy it by the polluting and raping of our earth and atmosphere. Praise and respect go hand in hand. A grateful heart cherishes every molecule of life as a blessing from God.

Return, O Israel, to the LORD, your God;
    you have collapsed through your guilt.
Take with you words,
    and return to the LORD;
Say to him, "Forgive all iniquity,
    and receive what is good, that we may render
    as offerings the bullocks from our stalls.
Assyria will not save us,
    nor shall we have horses to mount;
We shall say no more, 'Our god,'
    to the work of our hands;
    for in you the orphan finds compassion."
I will heal their defection,
    I will love them freely;
    for my wrath is turned away from them.

I will be like the dew for Israel:
    he shall blossom like the lily;
He shall strike root like the Lebanon cedar,
    and put forth his shoots.
His splendor shall be like the olive tree
    and his fragrance like the Lebanon cedar.
Again they shall dwell in his shade
    and raise grain;
They shall blossom like the vine,
    and his fame shall be like the wine of Lebanon.

Ephraim! What more has he to do with idols?
    I have humbled him, but I will prosper him.
"I am like a verdant cypress tree"—
    Because of me you bear fruit! (Hosea 14:2-9).

Trust is hard work, and when we need it most we feel least capable of it. Hosea was coming out of a very painful human experience, the infidelity of his wife. Dogging through the ups and downs of trust betrayed and hope restored, Hosea speaks passionately of Yahweh's trust in the people and the need for them to trust in Yahweh.

Hosea's plea for the vision of hope resting in the power of God rather than in the power of humanity is persistent. Over and over he has warned the people that alliances with Assyria and Egypt, political deals formed at the expense of fidelity to God, and exclusive confidence in human solutions to problems won't work. Human ability alone cannot save, and all the treaties and horses available to them won't be sufficient to save them. In today's vocabulary Hosea would warn us against reliance on the amassing of nuclear weapons for security and the accumulation of wealth for happiness. Their fruits are violence, fear, and poverty. God's fruitfulness is peace and joy—beautiful olives and fragrant cedars, flourishing corn and good wine.

Trust in God has never failed in the history of the people of God, yet it often appears as the last resort. We try things our way first and end up being swallowed alive in our own destructive behavior. So did the Israelites at the time of Hosea. Fortunately for them and us, God is patient and persistent in love and in forgiveness. "I will love them freely." The choice is to trust in that promise of love.

> Seek good and not evil,
> that you may live;
> Then truly will the LORD, the God of hosts,
> be with you as you claim!
> Hate evil and love good,
> and let justice prevail at the gate;
> Then it may be that the LORD, the God of hosts,
> will have pity on the remnant of Joseph (Amos 5:14-15).

Amos was the first prophet to use the word "remnant" to signify the small group of faithful people from whom the Messiah would come. This word historically characterized the tribe of whom the Messiah was born. But the word has also taken on over the years a spiritual meaning, referring to those unknown, unrecognized faithful who diligently follow the ways of God without recompense or notice. Amos is acknowledging the humble people who, like Jesus, are rarely known in their lifetimes outside a small circle of family and friends. God is letting us know that popularity and numbers do not matter in the kingdom of God.

Fidelity to God and to the desires of God are the essential goals of every life. There is no divine election that picks a handful of souls from all humanity and marks them as the saved. All are given the choice. Not all are given the faith in Christianity, but all are able to choose between good and evil. The remnant will come from all nations, creeds, and races, and they will be those who do justice day after day.

They will be those who because of their choices have seen the wisdom of loving the good. As habits of goodness are formed, evil is no longer seen as a desirable object. For any habit to be formed, the action must be practiced over and over. The thousands of daily choices between good and evil gradually form a discerning heart. It is a sign of spiritual maturity to grow in love of good and hatred of evil.

At the time of Amos the promise was that the Messiah would come from the remnant. When Christ did come, few recognized or followed him because they had not developed the ability to love the good and hate the evil. Even the presence of Jesus was not enough for some hardened hearts. It is the same today. God is with us, but only those who have learned to choose between good and evil are open to see God present in every aspect of human life.

> With what shall I come before the LORD,
>   and bow before God most high?
> Shall I come before him with holocausts,
>   with calves a year old?
> Will the LORD be pleased with thousands of rams,
>   with myriad streams of oil?
> Shall I give my first-born for my crime,
>   the fruit of my body for the sin of my soul?
> You have been told, O man, what is good,
>   and what the LORD requires of you:
> Only to do right and to love goodness,
>   and to walk humbly with your God (Micah 6:6-8).

Somewhere in the theologies of too many faiths lurks the image of God as avenging judge or record-keeping accountant, an infinite Being to be feared and placated, at best a benevolent dictator. In Micah's time this was expressed by the exaggerated sense of offering sacrifices of calves, rams, and expensive oil to first-born children. Today the need for sacrifice for sin is less direct and more subtle. It shows itself in the disbelief that suffering happens to good people, implying that suffering of not so good people is a punishment from God for their sins.

Through Micah, Yahweh tries to teach the people what is the real meaning of worship. There are three things the Lord requires of every person: to act justly, to love tenderly, and to walk humbly with God. How profound and simple are these directives, proclaiming a sense of right relationship with God, others, and ourselves. Yahweh has taken worship out of the temples and put it in homes and businesses, in communities and government. Yahweh is rebelling against being relegated to the temple. This is Yahweh who moved with his people through the desert, who never wanted David to plan an elaborate temple for him (2 Samuel 7:1-7). Yahweh's place of choice was in the heartbeat of his people.

The worship Israel's Lord desires is honesty and justice in all things. A life lived in integrity is more pleasing to God than temple sacrifice. Nor does Yahweh want robotic creatures fearfully offering prized possessions to appease their divine Creator. Yahweh is tender-hearted and longs for all humanity to share in his compassionate tenderness. God is love, and love is of God. Anyone who expresses love in any way is sharing in God. Love toward another person becomes a holy act. Jesus will bring this to fulfillment when he preaches love even of enemies and then provides testimony by forgiving his own executioners. By that great act of nonviolence Jesus takes away every loophole we could possibly find to exclude anyone from our love and still think we can worship God in truth.

The final piece of advice in this trilogy of true worship is the most intimate: to walk humbly with God. No distant God had Israel, but one who simply desired to walk with them. Famous people tend to intimidate others just by their presence. It's hard to act normal with those who live in the limelight either by position or fame. Perhaps we keep the same sense of distance with God. But God wishes to walk with us, as trustworthy friend, beloved spouse, accepting father, nurturing mother. Elaborate rituals, expensive sacrifices, pretentious temples, and empty words are meaningless forms of worship. The true worshiper is the man or woman who knows God as Creator and Lover and is confidently and gratefully present to the ever-present God.

> For though the fig tree blossom not
>   nor fruit be on the vines,
> Though the yield of the olive fail
>   and the terraces produce no nourishment,
> Though the flocks disappear from the fold
>   and there be no herd in the stalls,
> Yet will I rejoice in the LORD
>   and exult in my saving God.
> GOD, my Lord, is my strength;
>   he makes my feet swift as those of hinds
>   and enables me to go upon the heights
>   (Habakkuk 3:17-19).

No one can do the work of God, especially the work of bringing God's peace to a troubled world, without abandoning oneself completely and relinquishing all the visible signs of success. If we demand proof that God's pathway will lead to the promised land before we embark on the journey, we will never leave Egypt. In every time and every place the essential ingredient is faith, a vibrant faith that can rejoice in the midst of apparent failure knowing that nothing of God ever fails.

It certainly appears to fail—Jerusalem fell, Jesus was executed, his followers were persecuted, Christians are martyred up to the present day. It's not necessary to feel overwhelming confidence in God's way; it is necessary, however, to be faithful in spite of apparent failures. It is this aspect of fidelity that is most crucial for those who assume the role of peacemaker according to

Christ's standards. Christ's way is to endure evil with love, to love the enemy, to forgive seventy times seven times, to believe in God's way no matter how few olives, figs, or sheep it nets us.

Habakkuk's final plea to the people was to not give up, to be faithful. The external circumstance of their lives looked bleak as they were overrun by foreign aggressors, and yet the call goes out to rejoice and trust. Christ's people are still being overrun by foreign oppressors and an idolatrous society. Yet the call is heard: rejoice, be faithful. Dare to hate violence and believe in peace. Exult in a saving God who alone is the source of all strength. Release the fearful hold on weapons that create the illusion of strength. Believe that staggering steps can become as swift as hinds' feet, leaping from pinnacle to pinnacle on God's holy mountain.

> Rejoice heartily, O daughter Zion,
>   shout for joy, O daughter Jerusalem!
> See, your king shall come to you;
>   a just savior is he,
> Meek, and riding on an ass,
>   on a colt, the foal of an ass.
> He shall banish the chariot from Ephraim,
>   and the horse from Jerusalem;
> The warrior's bow shall be banished,
>   and he shall proclaim peace to the nations.
> His dominion shall be from sea to sea,
>   and from the River to the ends of the earth (Zechariah 9:9-10).

When our ox has been gored, that is, when some wrong, intentional or not, has been done to us, we want vengeance. We claim the moral high ground and justify the hatred and/or violence we inflict upon the one who has wronged us. We send in the Marines or call out the troops, raise the battle cry, and proclaim that God is on our side. Sometimes we go so far as to assume our acts of retaliation are God's own justice. The Crusades, the Inquisition, the blessing of soldiers, war planes, and ships give the same message of divine anger justifying human carnage.

In contrast, consider the word of God through the prophet Zechariah. No conquering nation was ever led by someone on a donkey. Horses and chariots led the great armies of ancient times; tanks and stealth bombers lead in our day. The king of Israel will come on a donkey without a warrior's bow, meek and just. Meekness is a foreign word in the world of aggression and self-righteousness. It is equated with weakness, servility, or naiveté. Zechariah equates it with peace. Is it more courageous to face an enemy armed with a hand grenade than it is to stand there armed with love? To dare to look at an enemy as brother or sister demands a fearlessness and strength that far exceed that required to pull a trigger. One is defensiveness, the other vulnerability.

Rejoice and shout for joy, for the Messiah promised will come, vulnerable and open to everyone, replacing retribution with forgiveness, vengeance with kindness. Our Messiah will have the courage to ride a donkey into a city boiling over with threats to his safety (Matthew 21:4). He dared to disappoint hopes for a king victorious through physical strength and created a new world through a spirit of love for all. He knew peace could never come as a result of victory in war. All that does is shift the balance of power until the next conflict. The strength to break the warrior's bow was the way to peace, not the strength of the bow itself or of the warrior using it.

The voice of history says it won't work. The word of God says, "His dominion shall be from sea to sea." Peace born of meekness and acceptance of all is the only thing that will work.

When he saw the crowds, he went up the mountain, and after he had sat down, his disciples came to him. He began to teach them, saying:

"Blessed are the poor in spirit,
   for theirs is the kingdom of heaven.
Blessed are they who mourn,
   for they will be comforted.
Blessed are the meek,
   for they will inherit the land.
Blessed are they who hunger and thirst for righteousness,
   for they will be satisfied.

Blessed are the merciful,
  for they will be shown mercy.
Blessed are the clean of heart,
  for they will see God.
Blessed are the peacemakers,
  for they will be called children of God.
Blessed are they who are persecuted for the sake of righteousness,
  for theirs is the kingdom of heaven.

Blessed are you when they insult you and persecute you and utter
every kind of evil against you [falsely] because of me. Rejoice and
be glad, for your reward will be great in heaven. Thus they persecuted the prophets who were before you" (Matthew 5:1-11).

If we had nothing else of Jesus' teaching but the Beatitudes,
we would know how to live as his disciples. Jesus is teaching a
gathering of poor, illiterate people oppressed politically and
starving spiritually. He reaches into their woundedness and offers
healing from the inside out. Rather than waving a magic savior
wand and taking away all their pain and suffering, Jesus brings
them to rejoice in the sacredness of the present moment. In their
poverty is wealth, in their meekness is strength, in their sorrow is
joy, in their hunger is satisfaction.

No one Beatitude can be taken as the whole message, none
stands on its own, but together they reveal the essence of the
peaceable kingdom. The whole Christ is in the whole message.
Although peacemakers are mentioned explicitly only at the end
of the list of Beatitudes, the ones preceding it lead up to peace.

The Beatitudes are a series of blessings. To pursue them is to
engage in a process of freedom. The first blesses all who dare to
drop material possessions from their soul's desires. Poverty is no
blessing; it is a result of sin in the world, but those who choose to
be empty in spirit open themselves to be filled with God. They
end up possessing all things. The second blessing frees those who
suffer pain from letting it be the last word in their lives. They
allow God to comfort them and to reach joy through the pain itself. The vulnerable ones, the meek, who claim no first place in
this world, will be the first in the kingdom. And they will be sat-

isfied along with all who feel the pangs of hunger for justice gnawing at their souls. Blessings of mercy are given to all who refuse to limit God's mercy, who confine no one to the tombs of their own sinfulness. The singlehearted, the guileless, will see God in all things and in all people because they are looking for God at all times and in all places. Their focus never leaves the face of God.

And for all who cherish these blessings, there will be the final one of peace. It will come because God graciously gives it and because Beatitude people passionately desire it. With the gift of peace comes the blessing of persecution. Peace is a threat because it challenges structures of greed and violence. The joy of the Christian is to be with Christ in his suffering. Even that will be freedom; perhaps it is the greatest freedom—to be so at home with Christ that intimidation and persecution are irrelevant. To human reason alone this is absurd. With Christ it is the dance of pure joy.

"You have heard that it was said, 'An eye for an eye and a tooth for a tooth.' But I say to you, offer no resistance to one who is evil. When someone strikes you on [your] right cheek, turn the other one to him as well. If anyone wants to go to law with you over your tunic, hand him your cloak as well. Should anyone press you into service for one mile, go with him for two miles. Give to the one who asks of you, and do not turn your back on one who wants to borrow" (Matthew 5:38-42).

Society recoils at these words of Jesus. Does he want us to be doormats that everyone walks over? Hardly. Jesus is teaching us the process of nonviolent resistance to evil. He is teaching us to respond to rebukes, threats, and intimidation the same way he did—by refusing to be victimized. Notice that there is no mention of fear or flight in this passage. Jesus Christ is afraid of no one or nothing, and he is leading his followers in the same way.

Mohandas Gandhi and Dr. Martin Luther King, Jr., both instilled a sense of pride and dignity in the people they were helping free from oppression. They taught them to be free of the yoke of the oppressor even before the laws and practices of society acknowledged their rights. First they became free interiorly, and then the oppressor had to relinquish the hold on them. Jesus Christ's teachings were the basis for both of these liberating men. This passage in particular speaks of such a practice of liberation.

Jesus tells us not to cower in front of the apparently powerful and threatening people who attempt to push us around. Resist the evil by refusing to react as a slave, a powerless person. Continue to act in love despite the threats, insults, and intimidation. Responding to evil with love confuses the perpetrator. It creates a crisis that can lead to the conversion of the abusive person, or it can break the cycle of violence by refusing to respond to hate with hate.

It is crucial to realize that Jesus is not asking us to tolerate violence passively. He is asking us to resist it actively with love. The former response makes us victims, the latter makes us free. Union with Christ always leads to greater and greater freedom.

"You have heard that it was said, 'You shall love your neighbor and hate your enemy.' But I say to you, love your enemies, and pray for those who persecute you, that you may be children of your heavenly Father, for he makes his sun rise on the bad and the good, and causes rain to fall on the just and the unjust. For if you love those who love you, what recompense will you have? Do not the tax collectors do the same? And if you greet your brothers only, what is unusual about that? Do not the pagans do the same? So be perfect, just as your heavenly Father is perfect" (Matthew 5:43-48).

Hatred and indifference to the welfare of others are the major cause of all conflict from family squabbles to international war. Sociologists and historians pursue more specific rationale behind conflict, but in essence it comes down to thinking of others as threats to our goals, ambitions, and security and then treating them accordingly. Jesus knew this characteristic of human relationships and he redeemed it. In other words, we have an alternative to conflict and violence. We are not boxed into the same old response of retaliation and anger. We are capable of being healed from the illness of hatred.

The prescription Jesus gives us is to love our enemies. This is not a complicated treatise of theology. It is utterly simple and extremely challenging. For many Christians, it is a foreign concept. For centuries we have been justifying our violence.

It is time to take Jesus at his word and to live his precept. The process of love of enemies is a lifelong journey, but we all need to be on the road. We begin by praying for the grace to love those who have hurt us or who threaten us in any way. It may take many months or years of prayer before we can stop hating someone, or it may happen overnight. Fidelity to prayer is the key.

Then we try practicing love of enemies. We consciously choose to refrain from speaking ill of others. We refuse to isolate ourselves from those we consider enemies or those who consider us an enemy. A simple "Good morning" may be the breakthrough. Perhaps others refuse to have anything to do with us. Our responsibility is to never close the door of our hearts or homes to them.

When enemies are determined by government, great courage is required not to jump on the bandwagon of war or threats of war. Violent solutions to problems are not an alternative for the Christian. This seems extreme, but so is all of Christ's message. Often we have no idea how to go about loving our enemies in situations that seem impossible to resolve peacefully. These are our annunciation moments, when we are called to risk entering into the unimaginable and impossible because God desires it. We are called to believe and trust in Christ's words whether or not we feel they are possible. The world blinds us, for Christ's way is the only way to life. The more common ways of violence and force are only illusions. They never resolve anything. They never heal or provide security and peace. Christ is God, and as God he knows what we need to live in peace. We need to learn, by the awesome grace of God, to love one another so that we have no enemies.

When the Pharisees heard that he had silenced the Sadducees, they gathered together, and one of them [a scholar of the law] tested him by asking, "Teacher, which commandment in the law is the greatest?" He said to him, "You shall love the Lord, your

God, with all your heart, with all your soul, and with all your mind" (Matthew 22:34-37).

Jesus reiterates in this passage the relational requirements of true faith in God. Love of God and of neighbor are intricately bound in the Gospel. The religious leaders of Jesus' day were trying to trip him into the box of legalism. Jesus answered their question by going beyond the limits of their concern. They were thinking of the more than six hundred laws prescribed in the Hebrew religion. They were ready to criticize Jesus when he picked one law as more important that any of the others.

Jesus skipped over their whole frame of reference and focused on the spirit of all law rather than on the minutiae of any particular law. God is the end of all life and of all our endeavors in life. Every law, every detail of every law is measured against the criterion: "Does it praise God and help spread the reign of God on this earth?" And Jesus has been emphatically clear that God's reign is recognized by the works of mercy: the poor housed; the hungry fed; the sick nursed; the imprisoned visited; the slaves freed.

Socially Jesus preaches that love of God cannot be separated from love of neighbor. Dietary laws, ritual requirements, and religious practices are not important unless they are focused on love of God and love of neighbor. Keeping rules makes us rule-keepers. Loving God and all the people of God with our whole heart and mind and soul makes us Christians.

> Then Jesus came with them to a place called Gethsemane, and he said to his disciples, "Sit here while I go over there and pray." He took along Peter and the two sons of Zebedee, and began to feel sorrow and distress. Then he said to them, "My soul is sorrowful even to death. Remain here and keep watch with me." He advanced a little and fell prostrate in prayer, saying, "My Father, if it is possible, let this cup pass from me; yet, not as I will, but as you will" (Matthew 26:36-39).

Can any of us imagine Jesus Christ coming to us personally, telling us of his pain and asking us to stay with him a while? Surely we could not refuse the Lord of heaven and earth, our beloved one. If we understand baptism, we believe that every person is Christ real and present to us. So the original question changes from imagining our response to Christ if he appeared to questioning our actual response to a brother or sister in sorrow. What do we do? How do we treat them? Do we run from others' grief, or do we stay a while and pray with them?

Christ is asking his disciples to help him through his night of agony so that both he and they might be strengthened for the grief that awaits them. People committed to peace are not meant to flee all places and situations of violence to escape the terror of it. Like Christ we pray our way through the fear, believing with Christ in loving in the face of personal danger. Many say that this is ridiculous, that no one can face such a threat with love and hope. Christ did in the garden; and because Christ lives in us, we also can do it.

Christ tells us how to prepare—to pray always, especially when fear tries to immobilize our hearts. Fear is the great obstacle to peace. Until we can face down our fears, we cannot be people of peace. Again Christ is our model. Over and over in the Garden of Gethsemane Jesus prayed in the grip of fear so overwhelming that he sweat blood. Yet he prayed and surrendered over and over. In time he was strengthened. He woke up his less faithful disciples to let them know it was time. He was ready to go with the Father in love. The acts of hatred toward him would kill him, but they could not shatter his faith or his love. He would endure evil with love, forgiving and even excusing his executioners from the cross.

People of peace must prepare ahead of time for violence by praying the prayer of Christ, complete surrender and constant awareness of the loving embrace of the Father at all times, especially at times of great fear. Christ is stronger than fear, and love is stronger than death. A Christian lives this faith reality in the throes of violence and threats because Christ did it before us and still remains with us as our source of strength.

———————

But early in the morning he arrived again in the temple area, and all the people started coming to him, and he sat down and taught them. Then the scribes and the Pharisees brought a woman who had been caught in adultery and made her stand in the middle. They said to him, "Teacher, this woman was caught in the very act of committing adultery. Now in the law, Moses commanded us to stone such women. So what do you say?" They said this to test him, so that they could have some charge to bring against him. Jesus bent down and began to write on the ground with his finger. But when they continued asking him, he straightened up and said to them, "Let the one among you who is without sin be the first to throw a stone at her." Again he bent down and wrote on the ground. And in response, they went away one by one, beginning with the elders. So he was left alone with the woman before him. Then Jesus straightened up and said to her, "Woman, where are they? Has no one condemned you?" She replied, "No one, sir." Then Jesus said, "Neither do I condemn you. Go, [and] from now on do not sin any more" (John 8:2-11).

Debate about the death penalty is raging around the world. Abolishing it is a requirement for countries to join the European Common Community. Human rights activists are calling for a worldwide moratorium. Numerous studies have shown state execution to be flawed wherever it is used. The poor suffer the most, without access to the legal benefits of the wealthy. The United States is one of only six countries that have executed child offenders since 1990 and has executed more such prisoners (ten) than the other five countries combined (nine) during this period.[2] Church leaders, in particular Catholic leaders, have spoken against it publicly for years. Yet the reality not only exists but is encouraged by many who consider themselves good Christians.

Fear of crime and outrage at acts of brutal violence often lead people to cry for the death penalty. It is never simple emotionally or psychologically to face objective evil, resist it, condemn it, and yet not step over the line of condemning the perpetrator of the evil. Difficult questions of our own motivation must accompany reflection on this serious topic. We must honestly face the revenge if that is what is in our hearts. With all the debate and the rhetoric surrounding capital punishment, it is

[2] Amnesty International USA.

necessary for each individual to find the response of Christ in his or her own heart and then to stand for this response. It is not the newspaper and the television that are the main sources for decision-making. The gospel—the life and teachings of Jesus Christ—is the moral standard for a Christian.

Not every moral issue of today was part of Jesus' lived experience when he walked this earth. But the death penalty was! Jesus was asked his opinion of it in the case of the woman caught in adultery. Reflection on Jesus' response leads to reflection on our response today to the same question. The only difference today is that a needle has replaced the stone.

SECTION FOUR

The Reward

The Lord GOD has given me
   a well-trained tongue,
That I might know how to speak to the weary
   a word that will rouse them.
Morning after morning
   he opens my ear that I may hear (Isaiah 50:4).

As we begin to reflect on the results of an active relationship with God, the most obvious reward of such a life is that the dialogue with God continues. The prophet of peace, the spokesperson for God's eternal peace, rises day after day to hear the word of peace anew. Prayer is the word given to this dialogue with God. Perseverance in daily prayer is a gift both given and received. Fidelity to daily prayer is a gift from God, and it is a gift to God. The lines cannot be separated. And this daily prayer becomes the basis for continual fidelity to daily acts of peace.

Rarely will peace be the result of major breakthroughs between people or countries. Even when there is a peace treaty signed, the reality of peace happening depends more on the people living it than on the paper on which it was written. It is the day-to-day living out of the gifts of the Holy Spirit—patience, joy, kindness, truthfulness—that brings lasting peace to individuals and to situations of conflict.

There is no other way to maintain strength for the journey of kingdom-building than to cooperate with the possibilities of peace that reveal themselves in everyday life. To arise each day to speak to the weary, the ones broken by violence and shattered by discord, is possible only when hearts are open to the word of

God. God's word cannot be stale or belong to yesterday or last week or two thousand years ago. God's word is today's word, present to the moment, consecrating the moment, blessing every detail if we allow the sacred a place in us.

The simple act of worship of God each morning upon rising consecrates the whole day to the will of God. It allows for the awesome possibility of hearing new words and accepting new ways of being Christ's peace to the people who will cross our paths each day. It keeps the flame dancing. There are times when the fire will burn brightly and there are times when the spark is simply kept alive for another day.

Though the mountains leave their place
    and the hills be shaken,
My love shall never leave you
    nor my covenant of peace be shaken,
    says the LORD, who has mercy on you (Isaiah 54:10).

Not many of us sit calmly by while mountains move and hills shake. Violent thunderstorms, hurricanes, or tornadoes send us fleeing for safety and praying for deliverance. Violence among people usually causes the same result, except that we often add our own violent response. We fear the reality of any form of physical violence, and one probable reaction is to return violence for violence. A terrible murder revives a call for the death penalty for the perpetrators. A nasty word brings forth a torrent of verbal abuse in turn. The human rights violations of a foreign dictator justify another country's embargo that eventually starves innocent people.

In contrast, Isaiah speaks God's response to violence. Mountains may fall, hills may shake, others may hurt or kill you, but God's word of peace endures. Politically, peace is denoted as the time between wars. God is saying through Isaiah that peace for the one who trusts in God must be our response even during war or violence.

The covenant of God's peace does not sway on the winds of violence. It depends upon the promise of God, and God's promise will be fulfilled. So many in today's society feel overwhelmed by the spiraling devastation of violence. The prophet of God, while not denying the reality of the culture, submits to a higher call—that of peace. In the journey toward bringing that peace to every corner of the world, belief in the promise of peace is given those who can accept it.

For my thoughts are not your thoughts,
    nor are your ways my ways, says the Lord.
As high as the heavens are above the earth,
    so high are my ways above your ways
    and my thoughts above your thoughts.
For just as from the heavens
    the rain and snow come down
And do not return there
    till they have watered the earth,
    making it fertile and fruitful,
Giving seed to him who sows
    and bread to him who eats,
So shall my word be
    that goes forth from my mouth;
It shall not return to me void,
    but shall do my will,
    achieving the end for which I sent it.

Yes, in joy you shall depart,
    in peace you shall be brought back;
Mountains and hills shall break out in song before you,
    and all the trees of the countryside
    shall clap their hands (Isaiah 55:8-12).

News reports from television, newspapers, or the Internet usually bombard us with local, national, and international horror stories. It is a rare occasion when an upbeat story gets covered. In contrast to this atmosphere of despairing tragedy, the peacemaker lives in the spirit Isaiah is describing—joy, peace, delight. From all the many other revelations of God in Scripture, we know that this does not preclude sorrow and pain. But there is an overriding sense of hope in the spirit of one who tries to live by God's ways.

This contentment is not going to come in ways we expect. Peace and joy are fruits of God's spirit, so they come from God. God's thoughts are not limited to our thoughts; God's ways are beyond our ways. The great part of all this is that we are invited to participate in God's thoughts and enter into God's ways. In the course of a lifetime, in the course of a single day, we can ask God for many things—for health, for comfort, for employment, for courage, for safety, for friendship, for freedom, for food, for shelter. God hears every whisper of our heart. But behind every prayer we make, if we are to be like Christ, we always pray that God's will be done; that is the one important prayer.

Trying to live that prayer with our lives day after day, year after year, we move into God's ways and submerge ourselves in God's thoughts. Then joy and peace will be present no matter what the circumstances are. Peace comes when it is sought on God's terms. Joy fills us when we allow ourselves to be permeated with God's spirit. The rain will come, even when drought seems to be all around us. God has promised it. Our prayers may not be answered in the way we desire, but they are answered. Those who know God know that God's word is dependable. Abiding in that word is our eternal journey.

Once you were forsaken,
   hated and unvisited,
Now I will make you the pride of the ages,
   a joy to generation after generation.
You shall suck the milk of nations,
   and be nursed at royal breasts;
You shall know that I, the LORD, am your savior,
   your redeemer, the Mighty One of Jacob.
In place of bronze I will bring gold,
   instead of iron, silver;
In place of wood, bronze,
   instead of stones, iron;
I will appoint peace your governor,
   and justice your ruler.

No longer shall violence be heard of in your land,
    or plunder and ruin within your boundaries.
You shall call your walls "Salvation"
    and your gates "Praise."
No longer shall the sun
    be your light by day,
Nor the brightness of the moon
    shine upon you at night;
The LORD shall be your light forever,
    your God shall be your glory.
No longer shall your sun go down,
    or your moon withdraw,
For the LORD will be your light forever,
    and the days of your mourning shall be at an end.
Your people shall all be just,
    they shall always possess the land,
They, the bud of my planting,
    my handiwork to show my glory.
The smallest shall become a thousand,
    the youngest, a mighty nation;
I, the LORD, will swiftly accomplish these things
    when their time comes (Isaiah 60:15-22).

The United Nations declared the first decade of the third millennium a decade of nonviolence. They declared January 1, 2000, as a universal day of peace and called for the cessation of all wars for that one day. Many people are involved in educating the world in nonviolence for the first decade, but the day of peace didn't happen. People fought and people died from violence on January 1, 2000, as they have every other day for generations. How do we reconcile this with the passage of Isaiah? We don't. We simply, in great faith, believe that God will triumph. We do not judge success according to the statistics of the deceased or wounded. This is not a denial that there is no connection between God's plan and respect for life. God desires that people live in peace and security. God's plan is intended to be accomplished on this earth. We must never stop working toward the fulfillment of that plan of peace, but we cannot let the violence of the world measure God's power. God is at work in our midst, through every person who is seeking truth through compassion and mercy, through every person struggling for human rights and justice for all people.

In the midst of a violent society we discover the work of God. The loudest gun cannot block the voice of the prophet of peace. The voice of peace is heard through the cries of the distressed and the shouts of the oppressors. Those who know God and follow God's plan for peace receive this vision of peace. It's like having x-ray vision, making us capable of seeing what others don't see. Where others see wood or metal, the peacemaker sees gold and silver. Where others dismiss a small effort as futile, the peacemaker sees the hope of the future. The tiny bud will grow into the mighty tree that shelters many nations. Those who receive this gift to see as God sees are called to lead an often blind society into the same sight. — *How?*

> The spirit of the LORD God is upon me,
>   because the LORD has anointed me;
> He has sent me to bring glad tidings to the lowly,
>   to heal the brokenhearted,
> To proclaim liberty to the captives
>   and release to the prisoners,
> To announce a year of favor from the LORD
>   and a day of vindication by our God,
>   to comfort all who mourn;
> To place on those who mourn in Zion
>   a diadem instead of ashes,
> To give them oil of gladness in place of mourning,
>   a glorious mantle instead of a listless spirit.
> They will be called oaks of justice,
>   planted by the LORD to show his glory. . . .
>
> For I, the LORD, love what is right,
>   I hate robbery and injustice;
> I will give them their recompense faithfully,
>   a lasting covenant I will make with them.
> Their descendants shall be renowned among the nations,
>   and their offspring among the peoples;

All who see them shall acknowledge them
    as a race the LORD has blessed.

I rejoice heartily in the LORD,
    in my God is the joy of my soul;
For he has clothed me with a robe of salvation,
    and wrapped me in a mantle of justice,
Like a bridegroom adorned with a diadem,
    like a bride bedecked with her jewels.
As the earth brings forth its plants,
    and a garden makes its growth spring up,
So will the Lord GOD make justice and praise
    spring up before all the nations (Isaiah 61:1-3, 8-11).

The greatest reward God gives to those who are faithful is a share in building the kingdom both here and in eternity. The Lord Yahweh chose to anoint others to do the work of God on this earth. The covenant is forever, and the poor will hear the good news, those in bondage will be freed, the sorrowful will be comforted. In this divine act of salvation, God asks us to help bring it about. Cooperation with God in the divine plan of salvation, which is the promise of Yahweh given to Isaiah, comes to those who respond.

Who would not be honored if the President of the United States or the Pope personally requested assistance on the most important project either had ever undertaken? It would be natural to wonder why one person was singled out and not another. Most individuals would probably feel somewhat intimidated or at least nervous about accepting the responsibility. Going one step further, imagine the person in power taking the time to really get to know the individual being sought. It is hard to imagine anyone not feeling extremely special or refusing such an opportunity.

Take this scene and extrapolate it to eternal proportions. The one making the request is God, and the "project" is that of salvation itself. And this God is not regarding those chosen as slaves but as brides. The jewels of the kingdom, the fruits of the Holy Spirit, are bestowed on those who share with God the magnificent hope of salvation, lived in every creature made in the image and likeness of this same God.

> Thus says the LORD:
> Let not the wise man glory in his wisdom,
>   nor the strong man glory in his strength,
>   nor the rich man glory in his riches;
> But rather, let him who glories, glory in this,
>   that in his prudence he knows me,
> Knows that I, the LORD, bring about kindness,
>   justice and uprightness on the earth;
> For with such am I pleased, says the LORD (Jeremiah 9:22-23).

Jeremiah's main theme is that the knowledge of Yahweh is the essence of faith. Activism for peace and justice for the person of faith is knowledge of Yahweh. Wisdom, courage, and wealth are not important in their own right apart from the will of God. All wise decisions, all acts of heroism, all proper use of possessions are valuable only inasmuch as they flow from union with God. Kindness, justice, and integrity are present on this fragile earth because Yahweh is present and because people of God choose to cooperate with the intentions of God.

Pleasing gods has been a major preoccupation of people for thousands of years. In ancient times gods received sacrifices in an attempt to placate their anger or win their pleasure. There were gods for strength, fertility, sun, rain, harvests, peace, and war. The list is as long as the needs. The concept of appeasing gods didn't die with the revelation of God to the Hebrew people. Through their Scriptures their struggle to honor God was present. Often they fell into the trap of thinking that God needed or wanted sacrifices of blood or gold. Over and over God reminded them that he wanted their hearts and only their hearts. Yahweh wasn't interested in their monuments of gold and marble.

King David violated this desire of God. David decided that he wanted to honor God by an expensive temple of gold and bronze. Nathan the prophet explained to David that God didn't want that kind of temple. God's temple was in his people. David ignored Nathan and began the process of constructing the great temple of Solomon (2 Samuel 7).

Generations have followed in David's footsteps. There appears to be no limit to the expense of the churches and shrines built in God's honor. And what of the people of God? What of justice and integrity and kindness? Those are the ways to honor God. Those are the only lasting memorials to God. Union with God will teach us to erect these monuments in our lives and in our relationships.

I will be like the dew for Israel:
he shall blossom like the lily;
He shall strike root like the Lebanon cedar,
and put forth his shoots.
His splendor shall be like the olive tree
and his fragrance like the Lebanon cedar.
Again they shall dwell in his shade
and raise grain;
They shall blossom like the vine,
and his fame shall be like the wine of Lebanon.
Ephraim! What more has he to do with idols?
I have humbled him, but I will prosper him.
"I am like a verdant cypress tree"—
Because of me you bear fruit! (Hosea 14:6-9).

Planting a tree is not an experience of immediate gratification. Many take a generation to grow large enough for shade. The olive tree only produces fruit after many years of growth. Some fruit trees give fruit every other year. Young trees require constant care, and they are the first to suffer from drought or storm. Fruit trees need fertilization and pruning. Vines must be cultivated, and crops planted every year. The cycle of nature reflects the cycle of good acts. Sometimes a result of goodness is seen immediately; other times it takes a generation or more before any fruit is visible. Sometimes goodness seems to dry up or die without producing anything.

Hosea reminds us that fruitfulness is guaranteed by God; it will come. Every act of conversion and repentance will eventually blossom into new life for us. Perhaps because there is so much in each of us personally and in all of us communally that is in need of repentance, we don't celebrate the fruitfulness of goodness as it comes from God. For the people of Hosea's time, repentance involved turning from Assyria and Egypt for security. God promised the Israelites verdant cypresses, fragrant cedars, and splendid olive trees—the symbols of peace and happiness. They had no need of military or political assistance to achieve this. Yahweh would provide, and provide in abundance.

Nuclear installations, star wars technology, high-tech security devices are the horses and alliances of our day. We have no need for them. God will fall upon us like dew; we will bloom in beauty like the lily. Every act of conversion we make, no matter how small, bears fruit. Our roots of goodness are spreading under society to support the mighty tree of life in God.

> Then afterward I will pour out
>   my spirit upon all mankind.
> Your sons and daughters shall prophesy,
>   your old men shall dream dreams,
>   your young men shall see visions;
> Even upon the servants and the handmaids,
>   in those days, I will pour out my spirit (Joel 3:1-2).

To those of us born in the fullness of time, we know that the spirit God is promising to send is the Holy Spirit, one in being with the Father and the Son. To the Israelites in the fourth century B.C.E., the people to whom Joel was preaching, this was a major revelation that God would send the spirit. At that time in history Israel had no king. They were a communally centered people. To them, the spirit was the breath of life of a person. So for God to send his spirit was for God to share part of himself.

For those of us born after Pentecost, we know that God shared not a part but all of himself. We live in the time foreshadowed by Joel. We know that the Spirit is given to us in all fullness; and because of this Spirit we shall dream dreams and have visions. Only those who live in hope dare to dream or envision a new reality. Every baptized Christian is given the Spirit to do both of these. Imagine the world if the dreamers and the visionaries were let loose! Imagine the world if the Spirit of God was accepted!

The eyes of the young often reflect despair and hopelessness about their future. Some cannot think beyond the moment they are experiencing. Hope has not been fed to them. Reality has robbed them of their eyesight. At the other end of the age scale, the elderly are too often dismissed as irrelevant and out of touch. Because they move slower and reflect longer before any action, because they cannot always express themselves clearly, they are considered incompetent and their presence burdensome. Few are interested in hearing their dreams.

Consistent with Yahweh's predilection for the poor, God has time for those whom society dismisses. To those who feel undervalued and overlooked God promises dreams and visions. Through the expendable people of society, society itself will be redeemed. Dreams and visions are a far greater gift than anything made of silver or gold. All the money in the world cannot give the satisfaction of an inspiration or a possibility yet unimagined. The Spirit feeds us the impossible and the improbable through our dreams and visions, and then strengthens us to bring them into existence.

(Therefore the Lord will give them up, until the time
  when she who is to give birth has borne,
And the rest of his brethren shall return
  to the children of Israel.)
He shall stand firm and shepherd his flock
  by the strength of the LORD,
  in the majestic name of the LORD, his God;
And they shall remain, for now his greatness
  shall reach to the ends of the earth;
  he shall be peace (Micah 5:2-4a).

Of the myriad of blessings and gifts God bestows on us, Jesus Christ is the greatest. Micah foretells the birth of God's gift of Jesus through his mother Mary. With his birth, unity will be restored to the tribes of Israel. The Messiah will stand firm against all adversaries, not to lord it over them but to feed them. He will be peace.

The Messiah has come; Jesus is among us. But until the unity of the children of God is complete, we will not experience Christ in all his greatness. Division and lack of unity separate us from one another and from the One who is peace. Peace exists when all are fed by the one shepherd. Separate armed camps living side by side in a nonviolent coexistence is not peace. Different religious denominations merely tolerating one another's systems of beliefs without any efforts to meet and understand and reconcile is not unity.

The three major faiths of the world—Christian, Muslim, and Jewish—all are children of the book, all share belief in one God, all are children of Abraham. Almost every war the world has ever fought has involved people of those faiths killing and hating one another—children of the same father, children of the same God, acting as if unity with one another was not a necessary requirement of worship of the one God.

Micah gives us hope. The presence of Jesus the Good Shepherd promises unity among all people. We live in that promise and live in expectation that it will come about in our day with the help of our efforts. A false sense of ecumenism that stops at tolerance may be a step forward for some, but it is not the promise of the Messiah. The Messiah will be peace; Jesus is peace. We believe that in Jesus we will all be one in faith and in love.

Shout for joy, O daughter Zion!
  sing joyfully, O Israel!
Be glad and exult with all your heart,
  O daughter Jerusalem!
The LORD has removed the judgment against you,
  he has turned away your enemies;
The King of Israel, the LORD, is in your midst,
  you have no further misfortune to fear.
On that day, it shall be said to Jerusalem:
  Fear not, O Zion, be not discouraged!
The LORD, your God, is in your midst,
  a mighty savior;

He will rejoice over you with gladness,
  and renew you in his love,
He will sing joyfully because of you,
  as one sings at festivals (Zephaniah 3:14-18a).

Surrender to God opens our hearts to accept the gracious abundance of God's overwhelming love for us. In the presence of that love, fear leaves us. No enemy binds us or blinds us. God is in our midst loving us and rejoicing in us. We realize that God delights in us and rejoices over us. God who alone is worthy of exultation is exulting in us. God is dancing with joy at our very existence and proclaiming a festival in our honor.

If we understand Hebrew worship, their singing of the psalms and their dancing before the temple of Yahweh, we can appreciate Micah's description of Yahweh's response. The tambourines, flute, lyre, and harp proclaimed the joy of the Hebrew people's worship of their God. They danced and played for him. In slavery their harps were hung on trees, and sorrow kept their feet from dancing. Only in freedom could they worship as they desired. Micah is telling us that the time of slavery is over. Dancing and music fill the air, and Yahweh himself is doing the dancing, striking the harp, and singing the songs—so great is Yahweh's delight in his people. It is Yahweh who is proclaiming the festival. It is Yahweh who is freeing the people. It is Yahweh who is revealing the beauty of the people chosen for his own.

Children brought up in love learn to be loving adults. With God, even those who suffer abuse and degradation in any form can be healed and freed from the bonds of self-hatred. God's promise of freedom and God's desire to rejoice and delight in our being exceed the woundedness of our bodies and psyches. God respects who we are at the same time that he takes us beyond our human limitations. Every man, woman, and child is created in the image of God, and because of this every man, woman, and child is capable of being the object of God's delight.

At that time Jesus said in reply, "I give praise to you, Father, Lord of heaven and earth, for although you have hidden these things from the wise and the learned you have revealed them to the childlike. Yes, Father, such has been your gracious will. All things have been handed over to me by my Father. No one knows the Son except the Father, and no one knows the Father except the Son and anyone to whom the Son wishes to reveal him" (Matthew 11:25-27).

Helen Keller lived a full, rich life although both blind and deaf. One day someone asked her if she could have either her hearing or her sight restored, which sense would she pick. Immediately she responded hearing, because, she said, the complete isolation from another human voice is painfully lonely. Until we are opened to the things of God, we are wandering deaf and blind to the most important realities in life. Isolation from the voice of God keeps us in a deeper loneliness than physical deafness.

When Jesus walked the earth, he cured many deaf and blind people. His ministry was to restore people to community, the community of one another and the community of the kingdom of God here and in eternity. All the scriptural accounts of Jesus' healings were done to people who actively sought his assistance and who believed in his power. Over and over Jesus commended the faith of those he had helped.

Seeking Jesus in faith remains the only way to be healed of spiritual blindness or deafness. Our lives have meaning insofar as we seek God. In this passage from the Gospel according to Matthew, Jesus reassures us that we do not have to be among those whom the world considers learned or clever to seek or understand the things of God. All will be revealed through the gracious abundance of God's generosity to any who open themselves as children before a loving Father.

The search for truth and wisdom permeates every society and age in history. Inner and outer journeys have been devoted to it, often consuming a person's whole life. The pursuit of truth is handed down from generation to generation, building upon or challenging others' results, imagining or creating new approaches to the goal of finding truth.

None of these efforts need to be abandoned, but Jesus promises that a simple, humble heart in a simple, humble person is all that is required for understanding the one truth, God. A child can understand the wisdom of God that a genius might never approach. All is gift, free, unearned, and unimaginable, and it opens deaf ears and gives sight to blind eyes.

"Come to me, all you who labor and are burdened, and I will give you rest. Take my yoke upon you and learn from me, for I am meek and humble of heart; and you will find rest for your selves. For my yoke is easy, and my burden light" (Matthew 11:28-30).

Sixty percent of the world's population does not have access to clean water. One-third of American women have suffered childhood abuse. One in six African women die in childbirth. Children in India's match factories begin work as young as five years old and work ten to twelve hour days. There are more refugees today as a result of war than at any other time in history. Factories in Hong Kong employ the brightest high school graduates in computer sound-board assembly that leaves them legally blind by age twenty-seven. One hundred fourteen million African women suffer genital mutilation.

How can we reconcile Jesus' promise of rest and support in life's burdens with this pain in society? We enter into mystery, a mystery that includes divine anger at evil and counts on human compassion on the part of people for their brothers and sisters in sorrow or distress; a mystery that allows God to break through human despair and hopelessness with infinite mercy and tenderness; a mystery that cries resurrection in the face of death. When Jesus Christ says something is true, then it is true on his word alone.

Jesus promises those who are oppressed by the unjust legal systems of the world and burdened by the results of the sins of others that they will find rest in him. Jesus is not talking only about eternal rest; he intends for people to receive that peace in time as well as in eternity. Not everyone will have that experience, but that does not mean it is not the intention of Christ. Free will and poor choices of others thwart the plans of God temporarily. But only temporarily. In the final moment Jesus' desires will be fulfilled.

Even when others continue to abuse people, Jesus will be close to those overburdened and in sorrow. In ways that are beyond human understanding and possibility, Jesus Christ carries the poor and needy in his tender arms. Never is anyone alone in suffering or anguish. Jesus takes on everyone's yoke and everyone's burden as his. He carries them and us. In the arms of Christ everything in our arms is light and easy. Mystery upon mystery.

Then Peter said to him in reply, "We have given up everything and followed you. What will there be for us?" Jesus said to them, "Amen, I say to you that you who have followed me, in the new age, when the Son of Man is seated on his throne of glory, will yourselves sit on twelve thrones, judging the twelve tribes of Israel. And everyone who has given up houses or brothers or sisters or father or mother or children or lands for the sake of my name will receive a hundred times more, and will inherit eternal life. But many who are first will be last, and the last will be first" (Matthew 19:27-30).

To understand this passage of Matthew, just have a conversation with someone who has followed Christ and lived his teachings in an extreme way—a priest or religious who is faithful and happy, a mother or father who has sacrificed wealth and personal goals for children, an employee who has abandoned a higher-paying job for one that serves others, a peacemaker who has stood up to injustice. To others whose values don't include Christ, these people may not look as if they are getting the hundredfold. But to those who value inner strength and peace, integrity and wholeness, the rewards are present even in the midst of trial and persecution.

Those who follow Christ and try to live his precepts of love of enemy and mercy toward all experience joy greater than any pain. They may be and usually are materially poor, undervalued and overlooked in society, considered dreamers and visionaries in a pejorative sense. God provides them with abundant blessings. They experience an abiding sense of meaning in their lives. This certainly does not mean that doubt and a feeling of emptiness are not also present. In the midst of it, however, is the knowledge of God penetrating every fiber of being and moment of existence.

No trial, no loss, no failure can touch the fulfillment God gives to those who are faithful. A life of fidelity is its own reward. Psychologically it is healthy; spiritually it is nourishing. Such a life includes mistakes and sin, but it relies on God no matter what else happens. Eventually such a life instills in us a conviction that God also relies on us. How incredible to think, experience, and know that the infinite God who created heaven and earth is by our side constantly supporting us, loving us, and using us to bring about the reign of God on this earth.

> When he was going back to the city in the morning, he was hungry. Seeing a fig tree by the road, he went over to it, but found nothing on it except leaves. And he said to it, "May no fruit ever come from you again." And immediately the fig tree withered. When the disciples saw this, they were amazed and said, "How was it that the fig tree withered immediately?" Jesus said to them in reply, "Amen, I say to you, if you have faith and do not waver, not only will you do what has been done to the fig tree, but even if you say to this mountain, 'Be lifted up and thrown into the sea,' it will be done. Whatever you ask for in prayer with faith, you will receive" (Matthew 21:18-22).

Most people would have a hard time believing that God answers every prayer. When someone is sick or in danger, we pray for their health or their safety. If a person gets better or returns home in one piece, we credit God for answering our prayers. If the ill person gets worse and dies or tragedy strikes the person in danger, we yell at God and assume that our prayers were not answered.

This passage from Matthew doesn't make sense if we think this way. Can we really believe that we will receive everything we ask for in prayer? If our faith is strong, then the answer is yes. One of the benefits of faith is more faith and stronger faith. Every time we reach a little further into our reserve of faith and stretch our trust in God, we become stronger in faith.

A marathon runner does not get up one morning and decide to run 26.2 miles. It would be impossible even for a strong,
physically fit person. The only way to run a marathon is to train
for many months. Stretching exercises, increasingly long runs,
daily runs, good food, sufficient rest, and a plan of preparation
are all essential ingredients of a marathon race. The spiritual life
mirrors the physical. To increase our faith, we need to exercise it,
believe when things don't work out as we would like them to,
trust when the desired result doesn't occur. Eventually the spiritual muscles are able to go a further distance and respond to a
greater demand.

Then we become marathoners in God. We believe in God's
abiding, consoling, supporting presence in crises that threaten to
overwhelm us with terror. The waves of pain are kept at bay by
the inherent knowledge that God is present to us, and in that
presence is the answer to every prayer. We begin to find answers
in ways and places we would never have looked before. We begin
to look at mountains that need to be moved in the same way a
marathoner looks at hills and long miles alone. We simply begin
and take the first step. The distant obstacle or challenge will be
faced when it is the present moment. Then the power of God will
provide the necessary strength, and the light of the Holy Spirit
will send the wisdom to take that step in faith. The miracle is not
that things turn out the way we want but that we learn to find
God in whatever happens.

The eleven disciples went to Galilee, to the mountain to which
Jesus had ordered them. When they saw him, they worshiped, but
they doubted. Then Jesus approached and said to them, "All power
in heaven and on earth has been given to me. Go, therefore, and
make disciples of all nations, baptizing them in the name of the
Father, and of the Son, and of the holy Spirit, teaching them to observe all that I have commanded you. And behold, I am with you
always, until the end of the age" (Matthew 28:16-20).

How encouraging those first disciples of Jesus are to us!
They witnessed Jesus in flesh and blood. They saw his healing

miracles. They heard him preach and watched him pray. They laughed and cried with him, and yet they doubted. They were so human and so like us. We believe and doubt, trust and fear, love and act selfishly. Jesus knew his followers. He knew their virtues and their sins, and he used them just as they were. He sent them out beyond the familiar to all the world.

To take Christ and his message seriously is to be open to being moved beyond the known into the new and untried where no one is a stranger to anyone else because all are one in Christ. Following Christ, sitting at his feet, and learning from him lead us into places inside and outside that we could never go on our own. Anyone who travels the world can go to every corner of the earth. But traveling with Christ brings us into new regions of our minds and hearts. We embrace people others see as foreign; we abandon places that others call home. We are sent into the whole world. No one, friend or enemy, is beyond the call of Christ. Christ desires everyone to be one with him, and he sends us to gather them up and let them know his desires.

Following Christ leads us to be Christ, to bear the name of Father, Son, and Spirit to city and country, to village and hut. We educate ourselves and embrace the career and vocation unique to each of us. At the same time, from this diversity comes one purpose and one pursuit. We all share the one vocation: to bring Christ to all people. We are all called as Mary was at the annunciation. God asks each of us if we will bear Christ to others in this world. Like Mary, we are being asked to surrender all we are and all we will ever be. Being asked is God's great gift to us. Responding is God's gift, but it is also our gift to God.

Jesus began to say to them, "See that no one deceives you. Many will come in my name saying, 'I am he,' and they will deceive many. When you hear of wars and reports of wars do not be alarmed; such things must happen, but it will not yet be the end. Nation will rise against nation and kingdom against kingdom. There will be earthquakes from place to place and there will be famines. These are the beginnings of the labor pains.

"Watch out for yourselves. They will hand you over to the courts. You will be beaten in synagogues. You will be arraigned before governors and kings because of me, as a witness before them. But the gospel must first be preached to all nations. When they lead you away and hand you over, do not worry beforehand about what you are to say. But say whatever will be given to you at that hour. For it will not be you who are speaking but the holy Spirit. Brother will hand over brother to death, and the father his child; children will rise up against parents and have them put to death. You will be hated by all because of my name. But the one who perseveres to the end will be saved" (Mark 13:5-13).

To those who do not know God intimately, this reward looks like the booby prize. Persecution, abandonment by family and friends, beatings in synagogues, hostile officials, and betrayal hardly sound like great benefits. Doesn't God care if we suffer because of him? Does God want us to be miserable in order to prove our love? The answer to these questions is yes and no. Yes, God cares when we suffer, and no, God does not want us to be miserable.

Although the suffering may be what grabs our attention when we first read these sentences, the point of the passage is the assurance of God's protection whenever we witness to the Good News. That is indeed good news. God is all-powerful, almighty, all-knowing, and more. This God is promising us a fail-safe security system—twenty-four hours a day, seven days a week, plus all eternity when time is absorbed into it.

This promise of security is essential for someone who aspires to a life of nonviolence. If fear of future harm from an enemy or need for retaliation for past harm consumes a person, then it is impossible to live in nonviolent love. A key factor in espousing nonviolence is confidence in God's constant protection even when physical danger is present, even when our bodies suffer physical abuse or death. If we allow those who hurt us to have the final word, then we will not be able to endure evil with love. Only when God is so present to us that death itself holds no sting can we embrace the one who does evil to us with the same love that Christ embraces the evildoer. When we do this, we are truly free and witnessing to the Good News of salvation for all people.

As they were proceeding on their journey someone said to him, "I will follow you wherever you go." Jesus answered him, "Foxes have dens and birds of the sky have nests, but the Son of Man has nowhere to rest his head." And to another he said, "Follow me." But he replied, "[Lord,] let me go first and bury my father." But he answered him, "Let the dead bury their dead. But you, go and proclaim the kingdom of God." And another said, "I will follow you, Lord, but first let me say farewell to my family at home." [To him] Jesus said, "No one who sets a hand to the plow and looks to what was left behind is fit for the kingdom of God" (Luke 9:57-62).

Anything Christ asks of us, Christ gives us the ability to do. Jesus lets his apostles and us know the hardships of discipleship. There is nowhere to call home but the heart of Christ. No demands of daily life can take precedence over the demands of the kingdom of God. It is first and only in priority for the disciple of Christ. Reality and personal obligations demand accountability from us. But what Christ is saying is that all other responsibilities are of value only when they are part of the kingdom plan.

We work to support a family. In Christ we work to further the kingdom of God and to raise our family in the same pursuit. If we are a mechanic, we fix machines to further the kingdom of God. If we teach, we educate for the kingdom, regardless of the subject we teach. If we serve the poor, we serve Christ. If we suffer debilitating illness, we suffer for the kingdom. Everything is trivial unless it builds the kingdom of God.

God's great gift of freedom comes to those who live like this. Nothing can take the joy of kingdom-making from them. Their concern is fidelity, not success. They learn to measure in God's way, which is by the fruits of love, kindness, compassion, tolerance, peace, and joy. There will be persecution and suffering, but there will also be freedom and gratitude to God. The unimportant realities of life will remain unimportant. This is the blessing of leaving everything for Christ—nothing material can consume us, so we remain free. So many are bogged down with trivial pursuits. Their lives are stressful and insecure, always measuring themselves against others' standards of acceptance. They lose themselves in the process. Christ is telling

his apostles to choose to lose themselves in him, and then they will
be free to be about the work of the kingdom, which is the only truly
fulfilling vocation for any person. To those who leave everything
without looking back, the kingdom of God is theirs.

———————

He said to [his] disciples, "Therefore I tell you, do not worry
about your life and what you will eat, or about your body and
what you will wear. For life is more than food and the body more
than clothing. Notice the ravens: they do not sow or reap; they
have neither storehouse nor barn, yet God feeds them. How
much more important are you than birds! Can any of you by
worrying add a moment to your life-span? If even the smallest
things are beyond your control, why are you anxious about the
rest? Notice how the flowers grow. They do not toil or spin. But I
tell you, not even Solomon in all his splendor was dressed like
one of them. If God so clothes the grass in the field that grows
today and is thrown into the oven tomorrow, will he not much
more provide for you, O you of little faith? As for you, do not
seek what you are to eat and what you are to drink, and do not
worry anymore. All the nations of the world seek for these things,
and your Father knows that you need them. Instead, seek his
kingdom, and these other things will be given you besides. Do
not be afraid any longer, little flock, for your Father is pleased to
give you the kingdom" (Luke 12:22-32).

Someone once remarked that the only people who don't
worry about money for rent, food, tuition, health care, and other
essentials of life are the very rich and the very poor. The rich have
what they need, and the abject poor are so far beyond hope that
worry has left them. These comments bear an element of truth,
but they tend toward the simplistic. Many wealthy people worry
about money, and many poor people never stop feeling anxious
about survival.

To read these words of Jesus while holding a baby with a
belly bloated from malnutrition requires faith beyond compare.
Try telling a homeless person struggling to keep warm with card-
board and rags during a cold winter spell not to worry. It's hard to
swallow God's admonition to be as secure in divine providence as

the flowers of the field when millions of children die of curable or preventable diseases. And what of the elderly who have worked hard for half a century and now find themselves abandoned and unable to care for themselves or pay for adequate care?

To all these crying pleas for help, Jesus responds, "Your Father knows that you need them." Is it possible to trust in God when there is no roof overhead? Because we separate God from daily life, we think it is not possible. We are accustomed to providing for all our material needs and to worshiping God on Sundays. In times of crises we call on God for extra innings. But most of us don't think that God has anything to do with our bank statement or tuition or electric bill. Jesus is trying to bring us to another level of trust with these words. He wants us to be so focused on the kingdom that everything else becomes minor by comparison.

Such trust doesn't happen by magic—it is gift and effort. It is developed through the actual experience of trusting. A family with five children had a custom of placing each newborn child on the altar at church on the first Sunday after birth. It was symbolic of the fact that the child was God's. Perhaps there is a need in us to create signs of trust. Grace before meals is a reminder that God is the source of all nourishment. A prayer over a paycheck or a job application could reorient workers to see God as their employer. When people are in the market for a new house, they look at desirable neighborhoods, commuting distance, potential school district, and price range. It is not uncommon for some to bury statues of St. Joseph to facilitate the selling of a house, but how few pray for guidance in the whole process. Advice is sought from friends, family, bankers, and real estate agents, but seldom is God asked for any input.

Jesus is trying to bring trust in God down to the nitty-gritty of everyday life. He is telling us that we cannot separate God from the very things that seem to take up most of our time. We are children of a Father who knows what we need. All we have to do is to learn to rely on him continuously and confidently.

"Amen, amen, I say to you, whoever believes in me will do the works that I do, and will do greater ones than these, because I am going to the Father. And whatever you ask in my name, I will do, so that the Father may be glorified in the Son" (John 14:12-13).

If anyone but Jesus told us we would do greater works than he, we would dismiss the possibility as ridiculous and sinfully arrogant. The words of Jesus need no defense, so we begin contemplating them by accepting them as true and as livable in our own lives. It wouldn't do much good for Jesus' credibility if all that he said was doable only by Jesus himself. Jesus intends us to do what he did and more. So let us begin to act on these words.

The world tells us that peace is not possible because of all the bad people. Society says greed is rampant, violence is a norm, and generosity is non-existent. Jesus tells us to do greater things than he did. And what did he do? He gathered a group of middle-class men, often dull of wit and slow of comprehension. With them he served and became friends with sinners of all walks of life—the white-collar sins of tax collectors and the no-collar sins of prostitutes. He raised people from the dead; he healed and challenged others; he taught them of the love of God, which knows no bounds.

If his words are true, we must be about the work of raising people who are dead in spirit to life in Christ. The marginalized of society—the young, the homeless, the elderly, the ill, the differently abled—are the ones to whom we are sent. High places in synagogues and churches and political offices are not of importance. A materially successful career is immaterial. We are called to be Christ. Before we do anything, can we ask ourselves if this is what Christ would do? That is the measure of our moral decisions, not mere legal right or wrong. The price of following Christ is a life without retirement. The work never stops. And the worker acts as if the plan of Christ for peace and harmony among the children of God is an achievable plan. Enthusiasm for the work of Christ is God's reward to the faithful.

"Peace I leave with you; my peace I give to you. Not as the world gives do I give it to you. Do not let your hearts be troubled or afraid" (John 14:27).

Peace is Christ's great final gift to us. It is given to us in the twenty-first century as much as it was given to those men and women who walked the earth at the time of Jesus' ascension into heaven.

Either Jesus was not telling the truth or we have missed the message. Jesus is truth, so the first is not a possibility. In giving us peace, Jesus expects us to act for peace and work for peace throughout our lives. Peace is not an option only for radical liberals who protest and end up in jail. Peace is an integral part of the Gospel.

At Eucharist, the only ritual prayer instituted by Jesus Christ, peace is mentioned in every prayer after the consecration. Somehow through the years we have become schizophrenic in our ability to separate the prayer of Jesus, the offering of his life to the Father for our redemption and peace in the world, from the actions of our daily lives.

Catholics are very clear about belief in certain moral doctrines but struggle with others. Abortion is wrong; there is no doubt about the Church's teaching on that topic. Despite three decades of statements against the death penalty by the bishops of the United States, 70 percent of American Catholics believe in it and see no problem with the Church in that regard. Jesus told us to love our enemies, yet many faithful Church members, including leaders, consider war a viable option. We are a Church in process toward a gospel of life.

Perhaps the gift of peace becomes a bit uncomfortable if all its ramifications are considered. Many times in Scripture God first seems to be an uncomfortable presence in people's lives. It takes faith to accept the discomfort, bear the squirming in our souls until God's peace leads us to light and peace for us and for our fractured community of peoples throughout the world.

"If the world hates you, realize that it hated me first. If you belonged to the world, the world would love its own; but because you do not belong to the world, and I have chosen you out of the world, the world hates you. Remember the word I spoke to you, 'No slave is greater than his master.' If they persecuted me, they will also persecute you. If they kept my word, they will also keep yours. And they will do all these things to you on account of my name, because they do not know the one who sent me. If I had not come and spoken to them, they would have no sin; but as it is they have no excuse for their sin" (John 15:18-22).

Persecution appears to be one of the promises of Christ to his disciples. It is clear that Christ is not desiring the persecution; he is simply warning those who follow him that it will come. To seek suffering or even to rejoice in it for its own sake is to be psychologically ill. Jesus would never advocate something that was unhealthy in any way. But to love Jesus Christ so much that nothing can inhibit following him is to expose oneself to the same suffering Jesus experienced.

Jesus was popular when he healed and fed people; he was not popular when he refused to hate anyone, even the oppressors. Jesus refused to use his divine powers to intervene in the political situation of his day to help his own people. Neither the Father nor the Spirit intervened to save the life of the Son himself. Jesus Christ was persecuted, and he was God.

By our baptism we become one with the person of Christ; we become Christ. When we live as Christ and refuse to cooperate with evil in any way, when political maneuverings and personal ambition have no place in the way we live, then we expose ourselves to the same reality that Jesus faced. We cut loose the mooring of the world and trust our very beings to the waves of God. Like Peter we walk on water. Anyone who loves as Christ loves walks on water. The illusions of security that rest on deals and money are shifting sand beneath our feet. It cannot support us. The one who walks on water knows that it is impossible without God.

Knowledge of the one who is the source of strength is the reward of surrendering to his arms. We may look unprotected and we may feel unprotected, but we are safe in the embrace of God. The suffering that happens because of our belief in Christ can never wrest us from his arms. And the day will come when we will rejoice in the suffering because we have become united with Christ in his suffering. His persecution and ours become one.

"I have told you this so that you may not fall away. They will expel you from the synagogues; in fact, the hour is coming when everyone who kills you will think he is offering worship to God. They will do this because they have not known either the Father or me. I have told you this so that when their hour comes you may remember that I told you"(John 16:1-4).

This passage seems very similar to the preceding one. There is, however, a nuance that bears attention. Jesus warns his followers that they will be expelled from the synagogues by persecutors who will claim the moral upper hand. Jesus knows that whenever people gather to form community for any purpose, even a religious one, there exists the possibility of disruption. Human frailties of greed, pride, ambition, and power can corrupt any group. In businesses the vocabulary of dissent and dissension are couched in terms of financial interest. In church groups the language is religious. Motives and actions are given "holy" labels. The end result for both is the same. When people struggle for power, some seize it and then expel the opposition to shore up the defenses within the ranks.

Jesus saw it all coming. He had firsthand experience himself. And he knew the same human condition that rejected him rears itself in every century and society. It is difficult for those who hold the power in any group to be questioned, challenged, or renewed in any way that threatens their power. Following Jesus entails the surrender of all power to Jesus himself. The conditions of discipleship inherently carry the risk of living in powerlessness within your own church. Jesus lived this way and he was God.

At the same time that Jesus prepares us for the persecution, he gifts us with the key to loving those who persecute us. Jesus says that those who oppress others, even in religious matters, simply do not know God, regardless of their position in any church. To know God is to be united with Father, Son, and Spirit in love for all people. Oppression and trinitarian love cannot coexist. If a time comes when we suffer in our own Church, we will remember Jesus' words of caution. In the remembering, we will be comforted and united with his own suffering. In this is peace. In this is the peace of Christ that redeems the world.

———————

> But we hold this treasure in earthen vessels, that the surpassing power may be of God and not from us. We are afflicted in every way, but not constrained; perplexed, but not driven to despair; persecuted, but not abandoned; struck down, but not destroyed; always carrying about in the body the dying of Jesus, so that the life of Jesus may also be manifested in our body. For we who live are constantly being given up to death for the sake of Jesus, so that the life of Jesus may be manifested in our mortal flesh.
>
> So death is at work in us, but life in you (2 Corinthians 4:7-12).

Death is the final test of our life. It frightens us, whether it is our own death or another's. St. Paul takes us to the limit. He faces squarely the risk of hardships, doubts, persecutions, and afflictions endured for the sake of the Gospel. Paul encourages us to be fearless in situations that usually carry extreme anxiety. This attitude of hope in the midst of doubt, peace in persecution, and life in death is the Gospel response to death in all its forms. Jesus Christ has conquered death, and because of that we need never fear it. But we do. At least most of us do. We panic at the diagnosis of a serious illness or tremble for weeks or months after a car accident. We don't feel fearless, and the reality of impending death can disturb us to the marrow of our bones.

How can we live in the attitude described by St. Paul? We cannot, but Christ in us can do all things. We are the earthen vessels bearing divinity. Pottery is fragile. It won't survive a knock to the floor or a bump from a heavy metal pot. And that's what we are like. No matter what color or shape we are, we are as fragile as porcelain. The realities of our lives could easily knock us down or bang us around; but they really can't if we embrace the divine treasure that we are by our baptism. We bear divinity in our poor, fragile, human vessels. It is this spark of the divine, the presence of God within us, that keeps us from being crushed or destroyed by death and the fear of it.

Gospel living may cost us the things the rest of the world values, such as money, fame, or power, but it liberates us from the one reality that everyone fears—death itself. God rewards us with eternal life after we die to this life. And God rewards us with freedom from the fear of death all our days. We live and breathe in God in this life and in the next. Nothing else matters.

Consequently, from now on we regard no one according to the flesh; even if we once knew Christ according to the flesh, yet now we know him so no longer. So whoever is in Christ is a new creation: the old things have passed away; behold, new things have come. And all this is from God, who has reconciled us to himself through Christ and given us the ministry of reconciliation, namely, God was reconciling the world to himself in Christ, not counting their trespasses against them and entrusting to us the message of reconciliation. So we are ambassadors for Christ, as if God were appealing through us. We implore you on behalf of Christ, be reconciled to God (2 Corinthians 5:16-20).

In wordless adoration we contemplate the person of Jesus taking the sin of the world on himself and redeeming every person who will ever walk this earth. Everything is new; everyone is capable of sharing divinity with God through Christ. Reconciliation enters the world, and Christ is forever in the process of transforming it. We are his agents of transformation, his ambassadors of reconciliation. St. Paul's words reflect Jesus' own message: Judge no one and be a person who reconciles one to another; in other words, be a peacemaker. Be one who looks at a person and sees the potential for goodness rather than the presence of sin.

Young children are natural peacemakers. Before they are taught bias and prejudice, they see people for what they are. Color of skin, ethnic differences, career, social standing, or wealth mean nothing to a child. They are attracted to persons who accept and respect them, who smile or laugh easily, who make them feel special. As adults our responsibility is to refuse to surrender to the biases and prejudices we have picked up along the way. When we see or are victimized by objective evil, then we assume the role of ambassador for reconciliation for Christ himself. We refuse to stereotype or blame or judge. We simply become Christ in a situation that needs him desperately.

Ambassadors to foreign countries are always conscious of the fact that they represent their country. If the president of a country called us up and invited us to be an ambassador, we would feel honored. The Creator of heaven and earth is inviting us to be an ambassador of redemption, proclaiming reconciliation to every person we meet. As ambassadors of Christ, we represent him. He came to bring us into peace with God and with one another. We accept our share in this work and begin to see peace not only as Christ's farewell gift to us but as our lifelong responsibility and treasure.

In the face of overwhelming support for violent defense of persons and countries, despite the almost universal acceptance of force to control, despite society's cry for revenge against the criminal, despite the lack of patience with the marginalized of our communities, Christ gifts us with peace. At all costs we cry to heaven and to the ends of the earth: "The old things have passed away; behold, new things have come" (2 Corinthians 5:17). Embrace the new, rejoice in the peace of Christ, and proclaim it by being the peace of Christ.